Maybe you feel like no one has your back, like you've been let down by people so many times that you've stopped believing in yourself. Maybe you feel like your destiny was written the day you were born, and you ought to just rein in your hopes and scale back your dreams. But if any of you are thinking that way, I'm here to tell you: Stop it!

—Michelle Obama in a speech to high-school seniors, 2010.

Michelle Obama
First Lady

Tanya Savory

TP THE TOWNSEND LIBRARY

Michelle Obama
First Lady

TP THE TOWNSEND LIBRARY

For more titles in the Townsend Library,
visit our website: www.townsendpress.com

Copyright © 2018 by Townsend Press
Printed in the United States of America

0 9 8 7 6 5 4 3 2 1

Photograph courtesy of Library of Congress
Prints and Photographs Division, Washington, D.C.

Townsend Press, Inc.
439 Kelley Drive
West Berlin, NJ 08091
cs@townsendpress.com

ISBN-13: 978-1-59194-523-9

Library of Congress Control Number:
2017953862

Contents

Chapter 1

"*I* can learn on my own!"

Four-year-old Michelle Robinson pulled the storybook out of her mother's hands and propped it in front of her face. She stared at the pictures and words with a serious expression. Marian Robinson smiled at her daughter. From across the small kitchen, Michelle's brother, Craig, grinned. He could already read, and he enjoyed reminding Michelle of that fact.

In fact, Craig, who was not quite two years older than Michelle, had learned to read before starting school. Now he was far ahead of his first-grade classmates. Michelle had watched their mother teach Craig the alphabet and then how to sound out words. Now, Michelle decided she was going to outdo her big brother; she would learn without anyone's help! But after staring at the strange lines and squiggles on the page for as long as she could stand it, Michelle finally gave in. She handed the book back to her mother, but not before shooting an evil eye at Craig.

Still, for all of her rivalry with her big brother, Michelle was extremely close to him.

"He was my protector and my lifelong friend," Michelle would say years later.

"We were so close, we were more like twins," Craig would agree.

In the small upstairs apartment on South Euclid Street in Chicago's South Side, the Robinson children had no choice but to be close— literally. The apartment had only one bedroom, a kitchen, one very small bathroom, and a narrow living room. It was really a space big enough for no more than two people, but Michelle and Craig's father, Fraser, came up with an idea. With the help of a friend, Fraser put up cheap paneling in the living room, creating two tiny bedrooms for Michelle and her brother.

"It was the smallest room I'd ever seen," one of Michelle's childhood friends remembered. "It was really more like a closet."

But Michelle never saw it that way. Her "bedroom" was barely big enough for a small bed and a desk, but by the time she was in the first grade, she managed to squeeze in a fancy dollhouse and an Easy-Bake oven. She often invited friends over to play with her Barbie dolls for hours, crammed together in a circle, giggling and laughing so loudly that Craig would be forced to retreat to the tiny kitchen for some peace and quiet. The lack of noiseproofing between their rooms annoyed both brother and sister at times, but sometimes they were glad for it. Long after Michelle and Craig were supposed to be asleep, they would press their mouths and ears up to the thin partition and talk, tell jokes, and muffle their laughter late into the night.

The Robinsons rented their apartment from an aunt who owned the building and lived downstairs. Both Craig and Michelle took piano lessons from this aunt. Craig was bored to death with the lessons and had to be nagged by his mother to practice on their secondhand piano. But Michelle loved playing. She'd replay songs again and again until she got everything perfect.

"We knew there was something special about Michelle when she practiced without ever being pushed," Marian later said.

Michelle memorized the theme song from the television special *A Charlie Brown Christmas* and performed it when anyone would ask (and sometimes, even if no one did). Years later, when Craig was the star player on his high-school basketball team, he would ask his sister to play the song to calm his nerves before a big game.

Like most kids growing up in the 1970s, Michelle and Craig spent a lot of time outside. They rode their bikes all around their neighborhood and hung out in a nearby park on the windy shores of Lake Michigan. They played epic games of Monopoly and Scrabble on Saturday nights.

Michelle was so competitive that Craig often let her win so that she wouldn't quit; he knew that if he beat her too many times, he'd no longer have a game partner. Craig and Michelle were allowed to watch no more than one hour of television a day. Michelle's favorite show was *The Brady Bunch*, a popular 70s sitcom that Michelle can still recall in detail more than forty years later.

"Somehow, she has managed to commit every single episode to memory," Craig said with a laugh in a 2008 interview.

Every summer, the family took a brief vacation at a small cabin by a lake up in Michigan or, when Michelle was a bit older, at their grandparents' home in South Carolina. A few times a year, there was a special dinner out for pizza on Friday night or even a drive-in movie. These treats, along with the fact that Michelle and Craig's mother was a stay-at-home mom while most of their friends' mothers worked, led Michelle and her brother to think they must be pretty well-off.

"Are we rich, Dad?" they asked one evening.

Fraser smiled, but didn't answer. The next day, instead of depositing his paycheck at the bank, he cashed it and brought home a big wad of twenty-dollar bills. He spread all the money on Craig's bed. Craig looked at it and exclaimed, "Wow! We *are* rich! I knew it!"

"Not really," Fraser said. He then pulled out a stack of mail that was typically kept on a small desk in his and Marian's bedroom. The stack contained the bills for electricity, gas, car payment, rent, and telephone. Fraser then put as many twenties as necessary for payment into each bill's return envelope. Then he put aside twenties for groceries and other typical expenses. When he was finished, there was a single twenty left.

"So, you get to save all that every month?" Craig asked. Twenty dollars still seemed like a lot to him.

"No," Dad said. "Remember when we get pizza or go to the movies? And our summer trips aren't free. In the end, there is no money left over at all."

To eight-year-old Michelle and ten-year-old Craig, the lesson may have still been a little confusing. In and around their South Side neighborhood, there were other children who clearly had far less. Some of these children didn't seem to get enough to eat. Their clothes were worn out. And both parents of these children usually worked, leaving the children alone or with neighbors after school and in the summer. Still, Craig and Michelle looked at the lone twenty-dollar bill that was left and had to agree, in low voices later that night through the partition, that perhaps they were not rich after all.

And yet the Robinson kids were very rich in other ways.

Marian constantly brought home books from the library for Michelle and Craig to read. They quickly discovered that good books were almost always more exciting than television (even *The Brady Bunch!*), and they spent much of their free time stretched out on the small front porch in the summer, cooling off and reading. Marian also saved spare change to buy extra workbooks that could help the children get ahead in school. Her plan worked! Both Craig and Michelle were given permission to skip the second grade when their teachers realized they were far ahead of their classmates.

Marian and Fraser encouraged their children to do their best every day, to strive well beyond "just good enough" in their schoolwork. They not only encouraged their children; they made them believe in themselves by showing them love and telling them how proud they were of both of them.

"I was always raised to believe I could do it all," Michelle explained. "That was very empowering."

"The academic part came first and early," Craig added. "Our parents emphasized hard work and doing your best. Once you get trained like that, you get used to it, and you don't want to get anything but A's and B's."

And while Michelle and her brother were raised to respect their teachers and other adults, they were also told to question anything, *anything*, they didn't think was right or fair or clear. They were taught to really think about what was going on rather than follow rules blindly. Fraser and Marian impressed upon their young children that always being a follower would get them nowhere. Also, being a leader sometimes meant speaking up and taking chances.

"I was not allowed to speak my mind or question authority," Marian recalled of her own childhood. "I couldn't say what I felt, and I always wondered, 'What is wrong with me saying what I feel?'"

Soon enough, at Bryn Mawr, Michelle's elementary school, teachers learned that they could not pull anything over on Michelle Robinson. Michelle also became indignant if she thought her classmates were being treated unfairly—by teachers or by other kids. At night, Michelle would talk to Craig about other students who were getting bullied or seemed to be having a hard time at home.

"I didn't realize it then, but I realize it now," Craig said recently. "Those were the people she was going to dedicate her life to, the people who were struggling with life's challenges."

Most of Michelle's teachers accepted and even respected Michelle's questioning, but one teacher was not impressed. After the teacher refused to answer six-year-old Michelle's questions, Michelle became angry. That evening, the teacher called Marian to complain. Instead of getting mad at Michelle or the teacher, Mrs. Robinson just laughed and said, "Yeah, she's got a temper, but we decided to keep her anyway."

The Robinsons knew, however, that simply encouraging hard work and freethinking in their children wasn't enough. They would have to set examples of their own. Fraser, in particular, set an example that made an impression on both his children, to their very core.

Fraser Robinson worked at the Chicago city water plant. He had worked his way up from being a night janitor to being one of the plant managers. Although he had never gone to college, Fraser had done well in high school, where he was a star swimmer and boxer. Standing well over six feet tall, he was a strong, broad-shouldered man who always seemed to have a joke or a story to make people laugh and feel at ease. But when Michelle and her brother were still very young, Fraser became sick with multiple sclerosis, a disease that affects the spine and muscles and has no cure. Victims of MS, as it is called, often develop difficulty walking as the disease grows worse.

Michelle watched her father struggle painfully some mornings to simply get to the breakfast table on time. Then she would worry as he took the steep stairs down from their apartment, one at a time, and shuffled to his car. Barely in his thirties, Fraser was forced to start using a cane.

"As he got sicker, it got much harder for him to walk," Michelle said in a speech in 2008. "But if he was in pain, he never let on. He never stopped smiling and laughing, even while struggling to button his shirt, even while using two canes to get himself across the room to give my mom a kiss. He just woke up a little earlier and worked a little harder."

Fraser Robinson never called in sick to work—not once. He never made excuses, complained, or even mentioned his illness. In fact, Fraser volunteered as a precinct captain for Chicago's South Side neighborhoods. As a precinct captain, Fraser went from door to door making sure that residents were registered to vote. Walking the neighborhoods was often slow torture for Fraser, but he did his best. The right to vote was immensely important to Fraser. It was worth the pain.

"Some of my earliest memories are of tagging along with him as we'd walk door to door," Michelle remembered. "We'd sit in neighbors' kitchens for hours and listen to their opinions, concerns, and the dreams they had for their children. . . . My father would make sure that everyone could get to the voting booth on Election Day—because he knew that a single vote could help make their dreams a reality."

As they grew older, Michelle and Craig developed a huge respect and love for their father. Disappointing him in any way was, to both brother and sister, perhaps the worst thing that could possibly happen.

"We always felt that we couldn't let Dad down, because he worked so hard for us," Craig recalled. "If Dad was disappointed in you, it was the worst thing that could happen in your life. If Michelle or I ever got in trouble with Dad, we'd *both* be crying! We'd both say, 'Oh my God, Dad's upset! How could we do this to him?'"

Many evenings, Michelle and Craig would stand at the top of the steep stairs, waiting for their father, throwing their arms around him in fierce hugs when he finally reached them. The two of them worried about their father even though he tried to keep the mood light. Sometimes, Craig would lie awake at night trying to figure out how to get his father out of the house quickly if the apartment caught on fire. But Michelle and Craig's admiration for their father overpowered their worry. And Fraser Robinson's steady and strong dedication to work and family made a tremendous impact on the quality of his children's character.

"Dad was our rock," Michelle said years later. "There were no miracles in my life. There's nothing magical about my background. The thing I saw was hard work and sacrifice. . . . Dad and my mom poured everything they had into Craig and me. It was the greatest gift a child could receive."

In turn, Michelle worked hard at school, studying at the little desk in her half of the living room for hours in order to get good grades. Craig also got good grades but didn't seem to need to study as much.

"Craig could do well on tests by simply carrying a book home under his arm," Marian joked. "Tests were hard for Michelle. I think she probably put too much pressure on herself."

In spite of her nervousness about tests, Michelle brought home mostly A's. She took advanced classes, even studying French and taking a biology class at a nearby college when she was in the eighth grade. The work paid off. At the end of eighth grade, Michelle graduated second in her class of more than one hundred students.

In many ways, the world that young Michelle Robinson lived in seemed fair and full of opportunities. She was aware, of course, that being black meant being a member of a minority, but her parents rarely, if ever, made bitter comments about discrimination. They didn't speak much about the widespread racial conflicts that existed in Chicago and beyond. Michelle had never really known why her grandfather, Fraser Jr. (her own father was Fraser III) had moved to Chicago from South Carolina many years earlier.

There were a number of difficult realities that Michelle had never had to deal with as a young child. But as the 1970s wore on, her eyes were opened to the hard truths of what it meant to be black in America—both for her great-great-grandfather and, more than 100 years later, for her.

Chapter 2

"What are those little houses behind the big houses?" Michelle asked from the backseat of the family's old Buick.

As the family often did on Sunday afternoons, the Robinsons were out for a drive around Chicago. Fraser and Marian loved to drive all over the sprawling city, answering their children's questions and telling stories about the history and people of Chicago. On this particular afternoon, the drive had ended up in one of the richest neighborhoods in the city. Huge mansions towered above carefully landscaped streets. Behind many of the big, fancy homes were tiny houses about the size of a garage.

"Those are called carriage houses," Fraser explained. "It's where the black folks who take care of the families live."

Michelle and Craig raised their eyebrows in surprise. They could tell by looking around that this neighborhood was completely white. That wasn't particularly surprising, but these rich white people put the black people who worked for them in little houses out back? That just seemed, well, *wrong*.

"Thus began a long conversation about racism and classism, integration and segregation, along with the history of slavery and Jim Crow laws," Craig later remembered. And woven into all of that was a lot of family history. In particular, Fraser talked about his side of the family.

Michelle knew that her grandfather, Fraser Jr., had grown up in South Carolina and then moved to Chicago. Recently, after his retirement, he and her grandmother had moved back to the coastal town of Georgetown, South Carolina. For the past three years, the Robinsons had taken the long trip down to Georgetown to visit the grandparents. Michelle had been surprised to find herself surrounded by aunts, uncles, and cousins. She'd had no idea that her roots were so firmly planted in South Carolina.

"Why did Granddad leave Georgetown if he had so many relatives there?" Michelle wondered. "Didn't he like it there?"

"It's a long story," Fraser said to his daughter. "It starts all the way back in the 1860s."

Before the Civil War, Georgetown was a town full of plantations. Plantations were large farms in the South that used slave labor to tend the crops. In the Deep South, crops such as cotton required many slave workers, because the crop was so difficult to plant, develop, and pick.

But no crop was harder to grow than rice, the main crop grown in Georgetown. When slaves were bought and sold, they particularly dreaded being sent to the coast of South Carolina to the rice plantations. Rice had to be grown in flooded fields, so slaves were required to dig a maze of complex canals that fed water into miles of fields. The digging was both grueling and dangerous. Fifteen or more hours of scraping, digging, and pulling out tree stumps left even strong young men bent and exhausted. The muddy coastal marshes were full of poisonous snakes and even alligators. And in the summer, the heat and disease-carrying mosquitoes could be overwhelming—and deadly.

Because growing rice required so many slaves, the population of many parts of Georgetown was 85 percent black. And when rich plantation owners and their families left Georgetown during the brutal summer months to escape the heat in the cool of the North Carolina mountains, the black population rose to 98 percent. In general, life was an unimaginable misery for most of the Georgetown slaves. However, their dense population and the fact that the majority had come from the same rice-producing countries in Africa made for a special community among these slaves.

Over time, the slaves in this area developed their own language and culture, known as "Gullah." In spite of the harsh conditions and mistreatment these slaves endured, they became strong and self-sufficient in many ways. They relied on one another, lifting their spirits as they created art, music, and a tradition of storytelling. The Gullah people of South Carolina have been called "a seedbed of black culture in the United States." This means that certain elements of black culture that still exist today began in that large slave community in Georgetown, South Carolina.

And in this seedbed grew the roots of Michelle's father's family.

Along a long dusty road about five miles from downtown Georgetown was the Friendfield rice plantation. It was on this plantation, and into slavery, that Michelle's great-great-grandfather, Jim Robinson, was born in 1850. Friendfield was a huge plantation with 500 slaves. Jim grew up on a dirt road named Slave Street on which dozens of crude, tiny cabins housed as many as eight slaves each. From a young age, Jim was forced to dig canals in the winter, plant rice in the spring, and pick extremely heavy sacks full of rice in the blazing late-summer heat.

Rice may have been a backbreaking crop for the slaves, but it was a serious moneymaker for the plantation's owner, James Withers. Withers and his family lived in a tremendous home just up from Slave Street. Pillars towered above the sprawling front porch. Red velvet curtains fluttered in the windows, and the doorknobs throughout what was known as "the big house" were made of shining sterling silver. A huge room housed a library packed with hundreds of leather-bound books. Slaves that worked in the big house often found their "master," as Withers demanded they call him, seated in his library, enjoying a book.

While Withers made sure that his own children learned to read at a young age, he also made certain that none of his slaves ever learned even one single word. Teaching a slave to read was against the law, and any slave caught trying to learn could be beaten or worse. Why were slaves not allowed to read? Simply put, slave owners were terribly afraid of their slaves becoming educated. They knew that if slaves could read newspapers, books, and the ideas of free black people like Frederick Douglass, their minds would be opened, and they might revolt against being enslaved.

"Once you learn to read, you will be forever free," Douglass wrote. He had secretly learned to read as a young slave boy, made a dangerous escape from a plantation in Maryland, and spent his entire life writing and fighting against slavery. This was exactly what the white slave owners most feared. Reading was a form of freedom that no one could ever take away. Many of the rich, white plantation owners refused even the thought of their slaves having *any* kind of freedom.

It is unlikely, then, that young Jim Robinson ever held a book in his hands. But during his life at Friendfield, he gained a different kind of freedom.

In 1863, after almost two years of terrible bloodshed in the Civil War, Abraham Lincoln signed a document known as the Emancipation Proclamation. This document proclaimed emancipation, or freedom, for all slaves in the United States. A terrible and shameful chapter in American history that had lasted nearly 250 years had come to an end.

Records show that Jim stayed on the plantation in Georgetown. This was not unusual. Many freed slaves, particularly the close-knit Gullah people, remained on the land where they had been slaves. Some worked as hired help, and others farmed a part of the plantation and shared their crops with the owner as pay, an arrangement known as sharecropping. Jim married and had three sons; the youngest was named Fraser. He was Michelle's great-grandfather.

Fraser also grew up on the Friendfield rice plantation (now a shared farm), and though there was no longer a law against reading, he had no place and no time to learn. There were no schools for black children, and young boys were expected to work all day. Fraser would most likely have remained uneducated if a terrible accident hadn't happened when he was ten years old.

While collecting firewood, Fraser fell and broke his arm. A simple break turned serious when it became badly infected. The infection was so bad that Jim Robinson was afraid his son would die.

Finally, Jim made the hard decision to have Fraser's arm cut off. In spite of being in great pain and unable to do the work that was expected of him, Fraser did his best to remain positive and cheery (a trait that would be passed along to Michelle's own father). A nearby white family, the Nesmiths, noticed young Fraser's good attitude and hired him to help around the house as well as he could with one arm. As Fraser worked, he often listened to the three Nesmiths reading to each other, laughing and chattering about the stories they shared.

Fraser began to wonder: could he learn to read, too?

No one is sure exactly how Fraser learned to read, but the story passed down in the Robinson family was that he was determined to teach himself, not unlike his four-year-old great-granddaughter many years later. As Fraser grew older, he worked at a number of jobs, never allowing his missing arm to be an excuse for not doing his best. After long days working in a Georgetown lumber mill, he spent evenings selling newspapers on the street corner. He'd often read the papers front to back. And as the years went by and Fraser married and had children, he brought home leftover newspapers for his children to use for reading lessons.

The oldest boy was named Fraser Jr. This was the grandfather that Michelle and her family now visited in Georgetown once a year. Thanks to his father's firmness about getting an education,

Fraser Jr. attended school until he was 18, earning his high-school diploma near the end of the 1920s. Fraser Jr. had been an excellent student, and he set his sights on going to college and a future full of success and opportunity. But in Georgetown, South Carolina, the only opportunity available to a young black man was work at the same lumber company where his father worked.

"He wanted a different kind of life," his daughter, Francesca, remembered. "He always had high hopes."

Following the Civil War, there had been a brief time in the South when freed slaves were given more and better opportunities. This was known as the Reconstruction period. The United States government set up guidelines that the Southern states would have to follow, which included the fair treatment of black people. Abraham Lincoln had hoped that blacks would eventually have full rights, equal to those of even the richest plantation owners. That was not to be.

In barely ten years, angry white leaders had retaken control of most local governments in the South. Then the hate organization called Ku Klux Klan was formed. The Klan and corrupt leaders terrorized and intimidated black people, making sure that blacks remained powerless and poor. The right to vote was taken away, black families were stripped of land they had been legally given by the federal government, and what became known as

"Jim Crow" laws were put in place throughout the South. These were extremely unfair laws that required black people to remain separate from white people in almost every way imaginable: in restaurants, theaters, schools, bathrooms, stores, and more. In some towns, there were even laws against black and white people having a conversation in public.

This was the world in which Michelle's grandfather, despite his "high hopes," found himself. He worked briefly at the lumber company, but when the Great Depression hit in 1929, lumber jobs for black employees disappeared. Fraser Jr. saw more and more of his friends leaving Georgetown for cities in the North.

"Everyone's leaving," a friend who was headed to Chicago told Fraser. "There are all kinds of opportunities for us up there!"

Fraser Jr. looked around Georgetown. In many ways, he hated to leave. All his friends and relatives were here. In spite of its unfair laws and discrimination, South Carolina was his home, and it was a place he loved. The sense of community that had begun with the Gullah people generations earlier was still strong in Georgetown and in Fraser's heart. Still, Fraser saw his friend was right—so many people *were* leaving.

What was known as the Great Migration had begun around 1910, and for the next 60 years, black people would leave small towns and rural areas in the South for big cities in the North, West, and Midwest. In all, more than six million black people left behind the unfair and dead-end way of life they were faced with in the Southern states, hoping to find a better world elsewhere. Michelle's grandfather would be one of those six million. In 1930, Fraser Robinson Jr. took what little money and belongings he had and, alone and barely 19 years old, left for Chicago.

Fraser Jr. had hoped to go to college and become an electrician, but in the midst of the Depression, the best he could hope for was any job at all. In time, he found work at a post office. A year later, he met and married LaVaughn Johnson, a young woman who sang in the church choir. In many ways, life was better in Chicago, but Fraser Jr. and LaVaughn still experienced racism and unfair treatment. White people did not want black people in their neighborhoods, so they made it difficult for blacks to buy or rent or even look at homes or apartments in white areas. Blacks were accepted only in certain areas, mostly in housing projects in Chicago's South Side. This is where Fraser Jr. and his new wife ended up.

Fraser Jr. was unhappy and ashamed to be living in the projects. He'd always thought that hard work would make his life better, but that didn't seem to be happening.

"He was a proud man," Michelle recalled of her grandfather. "He was very proud of his roots."

Sadly, nothing in Chicago seemed to remind Fraser Jr. of his roots. City noise rattled the cheap apartment he lived in, bitter winters filled the streets with snow and ice, and even the church he attended seemed different. The black people he met were not as warm and welcoming as they had been in Georgetown. Fraser Jr. worked hard and tried to fit into his new life in Chicago, but day by day, he became more restless. All his high hopes seemed to be fading, and it was becoming more than he could bear.

Into this discontent, Michelle's father, Fraser III, was born in 1935. Six years later, Fraser Jr. abruptly left his family, which now also included a second boy named Nomenee. Desperate to find a different life and get away from Chicago, Fraser Jr. enlisted in the army.

"Separated, without children," he wrote on his enlistment forms. To the army, Fraser Jr. appeared to be the perfect soldier—unattached and without any responsibilities tying him down. Within weeks, Michelle's grandfather was thousands of miles away from Chicago, fighting in World War II.

Chapter 3

Luckily for Fraser III and his brother, their father would not abandon them completely, but after Fraser Jr. returned from the war, it would be several years until he would move back in with his wife and sons.

"He'd come by once a year or so and take us to the circus," Nomenee remembered. "That was our contact with him. He lived a few blocks away, but only our mother knew exactly where."

Meanwhile, LaVaughn made certain her sons were getting as many learning and creative opportunities as she could afford. When he was only 11, Michelle's father began catching a bus downtown on Saturday mornings to take an art class at the Art Institute of Chicago. He was particularly interested in sculpting, and by the time he was in high school, Fraser was a talented artist. Michelle later said that if her father could have afforded to attend a good art school and spend time on his sculpting, he probably would have become a professional artist. In his high-school yearbook, there is a picture of a serious Fraser dressed in a suit and tie, carefully sculpting a human head.

Fraser was a quiet, hardworking teenager who understood responsibility even at a young age. In addition to attending school, he worked at a dairy and as a lifeguard in the summers. His father would eventually return to the family and support the household as a postal worker, but his father's absence had affected him. It was, perhaps, that absence that made Fraser so determined, years later, to be involved in and supportive of his own children's lives.

Michelle's father also understood racism even at a young age. Although the political leaders in Chicago tried to present the city as being a place where skin color made no difference, Fraser grew up seeing examples of how that was not true. He attended an all-black high school, and in the 1950s, the students talked frequently about the problems that black people faced.

"In those days, racism was not hidden at all," a classmate of Michelle's father recalled. "We knew how white people thought of us. We knew we *had* to do better than our parents had done. No nonsense—that was the key."

That was the key that Fraser Robinson used his entire life. After high school, he enrolled at the University of Illinois, desperately hoping he could earn enough money while in school to make it all the way through. But his money ran out. Rather than feeling sorry for himself, Fraser helped pay for his younger brother's college education. Nomenee would graduate three years later with a degree in architecture. Next, Fraser spent four years in the military in order to save a little money, serve his country, and learn some skills. When he returned to Chicago's South Side and married a young woman named Marian Shields, he was determined to provide a good life for her. Just three days before Marian gave birth to Craig, Fraser began working for the water plant, where he was employed until the day he died.

This long family history was told in bits and pieces to Michelle as she grew up, some of the pieces not falling into place until she was a mother with children of her own. As to her mother's side of the family, less was known, but there's a chance that Marian Robinson, too, was descended from slaves.

"There are probably thousands of one-armed Frasers all over this country, who, out of slavery and emancipation, because they were smart and worked hard, were able to lift themselves up," Michelle said years later. "This story plays a part in telling a bigger story. It is a process, of uncovering the shame, digging out the pride that is part of that story, so that other folks feel comfortable about embracing the beauty and the tangled nature of the history of this country."

The "tangled nature" of America's history with race relations, of course, did not end with the end of slavery—or even 100 years *after* the end of slavery. Only a year before Michelle was born, the celebrated March on Washington was held in Washington, D.C. More than a quarter of a million people gathered to demand civil rights for black people. It was during this gathering that Martin Luther King Jr. gave his "I Have a Dream" speech in which he famously said: "I have a dream that my four little children will one day live in a nation where they will not be judged by the color of their skin but by the content of their character."

That day had not yet arrived as Michelle Robinson was growing up on South Euclid Street. When the Robinsons had moved into the neighborhood in the early 1960s, they had quite a few white neighbors. But family by family, the white neighbors left. This was not a new thing. For decades, as soon as the first black family moved into a mostly white neighborhood in Chicago, their white neighbors began leaving. In 1949, the great black poet Langston Hughes had written:

> *When I move*
> *Into a neighborhood*
> *Folks fly.*
> *Even every foreigner*
> *That can move, moves. Why?*

"White flight," as it came to be called, was something Michelle and her brother witnessed firsthand. It was confusing to Michelle. Their white neighbors had never been mean or even rude to her, and she had always been polite and respectful toward them. But they didn't seem to want to live beside black people. Like Langston Hughes, she wondered, *Why?*

Many white people unfairly judged and stereotyped black people. Because for many years blacks had not been given the same opportunities and advantages as whites, many were poor. Some white people assumed that black people were poor because they were lazy or stupid. This kind of thinking produced racism. And racist whites automatically assumed that property values would go down the minute a black family moved in nearby.

"But that was not always true," noted Jesse Jackson, a longtime Chicago civil rights activist. "Often, blacks moved in and property values went up, not down. They were everyday working kind of people, and neighborhoods improved."

This was true for the South Side neighborhood where Michelle lived, but in spite of the safety and security of her neighborhood, seeing white people rush to move away sent a clear message to many of the black children who lived there: *White people don't like you.* This message had been loud and clear in 1966 when Martin Luther King Jr. had visited Chicago to speak at a civil rights gathering and lead a march through the city. Four thousand angry white people had shown up, screaming names at King and holding signs that read "King Would Look Good with a Knife in His Back" or "Go Home Nigger." As King led the march, the white mob chased him. Someone threw a knife that missed him, but another person hurled a rock that struck King and knocked him to the ground.

"I have never in my life seen such hate," King later said. "I've been in many demonstrations across the South, but I can say that I have never seen—even in Mississippi and Alabama—mobs as hostile and hate-filled as I've seen in Chicago. I think the people from Mississippi ought to come to Chicago to learn how to hate!"

This level of racism was still very much present in Chicago as Michelle and Craig were growing up in the 1970s. Their parents explained that most white people were not racist, but that discrimination was a real thing, and it could make you bitter and angry if you let it. They warned that Michelle and Craig had to be prepared to deal with some level of unfairness that went along with growing up black.

"Life's not fair," Fraser and Marian often said. "You don't always get what you deserve, but you have to work hard to get what you want. And then sometimes you don't get it; even if you work hard and do all the right things, sometimes you don't get it."

This may have been a disappointing reality to Michelle and Craig, but as Craig later pointed out, "It prepared us for handling life."

The Robinson kids were also prepared for handling life by their parents' constant reminders that they were as deserving as anyone, that they were smart, and that they were good people. Hearing this from an early age gave Michelle and Craig confidence. Fraser and Marian knew that confidence, combined with education, would be the best weapons against the discrimination that their children might face.

One form of discrimination that had been going on for a long time was segregated schools. When a school was "segregated," it meant that the student body was either all black or all white. In Chicago in the 1970s, children attended the schools in their neighborhoods. Because of white flight, this meant that most public schools did not include a mix of races. For years, city leaders had been fighting against segregation, but it remained a stubborn problem. Making the problem worse, schools in black neighborhoods often did not receive as much funding and attention as the schools in white neighborhoods.

When it came time for Michelle to go to high school, she wondered if she should attend the all-black school in her neighborhood. She and her parents discussed it. Both Michelle and her parents agreed that going to a school that had a mix of students from different races and various backgrounds would be a more rewarding experience. But that would mean attending a private school, and Michelle's parents didn't have that kind of money. Luckily for Michelle, a new type of high school, a "magnet school," had just been created in Chicago.

Magnet schools are so named because they attempt to "pull in" the brightest and highest-achieving students from all over a city. The new school in Chicago was called Whitney M. Young Magnet High School, and it offered advanced classes and far more opportunities than most schools. It also ensured that the student body would be racially mixed, since students came from all corners of the city. Many city leaders agreed that it was one of the best new high schools in Chicago.

"It was a grand experiment at a time when Chicago was considered the most segregated city in the country," recalls one of Michelle's classmates.

Michelle wanted both black and white friends, and she wanted to go to a school where she would be challenged, where her mind would be opened up to new possibilities and ideas. Michelle thought that Whitney Young sounded like the school of her dreams. But she had to apply to the school and take an entrance exam first. Next, Michelle had to be interviewed and considered by a group of teachers. Thanks to Michelle's good grades through the eighth grade and the confidence her parents had helped her build, she did well on her exam and impressed everyone at the new school. She was accepted. At just 13 (because she had skipped the second grade), Michelle was about to begin a new adventure.

The first big, and somewhat scary, part of that adventure was simply getting to Whitney Young. The school was on the other side of the city, and Michelle's trip there required taking two different buses and walking several blocks. She caught the first bus two blocks from her house in the winter dark before dawn. It travelled from her neighborhood into the roaring, skyscraper-filled center of the city. The next bus took Michelle to the outskirts of the city, to a rundown area scattered with abandoned brick factory buildings.

"Whitney Young was built in the middle of a slum," a teacher remembered. "It was barren, and there was a skid row just two blocks away where homeless people hung out."

In fact, the new high school had been built on a lot that had been burned out during rioting after Martin Luther King, Jr. was shot and killed in 1968. The school was named after Whitney Young Jr., a famous civil rights leader, and it was an impressive modern glass and metal building. In the dim early mornings, it was a welcome sight amid the empty, poorly lit surroundings.

This journey to and from her new high school took Michelle at least an hour each way. But, taking a cue from her father, she never complained. Instead, Michelle quickly made new friends who had to travel on the same buses to Whitney Young. Together, they giggled on the way to school in the mornings and did homework on the way home in the afternoons. If Michelle's parents were worried about their 13-year-old daughter, they didn't express it to her. Instead, they expressed confidence that she would be just fine. And she was.

Michelle made the most of every day at her new high school. She sang in the choir, ran for school treasurer and won (though she was very nervous about giving a speech in front of the entire school), helped with school fundraisers, and made the National Honor Society.

"I signed up for every activity that I could, and I focused my life around the goal of getting into the next school of my dreams," Michelle later said, indicating that she was already thinking about college. "It seemed like every paper was life or death; every point on an exam was worth fighting for."

Classmates remember that Michelle got along with nearly everyone and had a great sense of humor, even though she was fairly quiet. But, as always, if she thought an injustice had been done, she spoke right up. In her typing class, for example, the teacher gave her a B even though Michelle had done A work.

"I don't give As," the teacher told Michelle matter-of-factly.

"But that isn't fair!" Michelle protested. "If someone earns an A, he or she should get an A, not a B."

The teacher wouldn't budge, but neither would Michelle. Finally Michelle's mother had to call the teacher.

"Michelle is not going to let this go," Marian said to the teacher, knowing that Michelle was simply questioning authority the way she had been taught to do. Michelle's persistence paid off. The teacher finally gave in.

Finally, after four years of very hard work, good grades, and plenty of activities, Michelle was ready to apply to college. Craig was already at Princeton University in New Jersey, one of the best colleges in the United States. Still competitive with her brother, Michelle thought, *If he can get into Princeton, so can I.* She told her guidance counselor at Whitney Young that she wanted to apply to Princeton.

"Well, what is your first choice?" the counselor asked in a doubtful voice.

"Princeton *is* my first choice," Michelle replied.

"But you should pick a different school," the counselor said, shaking her head. "Your test scores aren't high enough. It's very, very hard to get into Princeton. You'll never get in."

Michelle heard the counselor's words, but she didn't believe them. She'd always aimed high, and she wasn't about to stop now.

Yes, I will, she thought to herself.

Chapter 4

" *The* world tells us not to search too high, and it puts all kinds of barriers for kids," Michelle Obama said in a speech in 2006. "The world says, 'You can't do this' and 'You can't do that.' I was told I couldn't go to Princeton. . . . As a black girl from the South Side of Chicago, I was told I wasn't 'good enough.' I wasn't 'ready.'"

When Michelle was told she couldn't go to Princeton, she became more determined than ever to get into the Ivy League school. Perhaps her test scores for college entrance had not been the best, but what about everything else she had done in high school? What about all her hard work? The admissions committee at Princeton sat down with Michelle. Craig was already doing well in his classes, in addition to being a star basketball player for the Princeton Tigers. In her interview, Michelle left no doubt that she was as able and determined as her brother.

"Michelle talked her way in," her mother later said with a laugh.

Out of nearly 12,000 applicants to Princeton in 1981, fewer than 2000 new students were admitted. Michelle was one of them. She was so excited about going to her dream school that she could barely sleep in the weeks leading up to leaving for college. And on her first day, Michelle walked through the 200-year-old campus with a proud smile on her face. She had made it! Towering maple trees grew beside beautiful old stone buildings covered in deep green ivy (which had led to the name "Ivy League"). In the dining hall, chandeliers hung from the high arched ceilings, giving everything a magical feeling. And Michelle's room on the top floor of the dorm building was a cozy and unusual attic with sloped ceilings.

Princeton was a different world from the South Side of Chicago in many ways that excited Michelle. But it was also different in ways that seemed strange or uncomfortable to her. For one thing, so many of the other students seemed to have a great deal of money. They were wearing expensive clothes that Michelle had only ever dreamed of wearing. And some of them drove very fancy cars.

"I remember being shocked by college students who drove BMWs," Michelle told a newspaper reporter in 2008. "I didn't even know *parents* who drove BMWs!"

And as she walked around the campus, Michelle

couldn't help noticing that there were very few black students. Some of the white students passing by even stared at her in a rude way. At Whitney Young, Michelle had had close friends that were both black and white; race had never really been an issue. But now, for the first time in her life, Michelle felt singled out by her classmates because of her skin color.

"Nothing prepares you to have somebody you don't even know ask you something like if your skin color rubs off," a college friend of Michelle's later said. "I got asked that all the time. . . . It was shocking. It was hard to be dropped in the middle of this environment."

Before classes even began, Michelle experienced the consequences of this new environment.

"Hi, I'm Michelle!" Michelle said with a warm smile, reaching out to shake her new roommate's hand.

"I'm Catherine," the tall girl with two suitcases said with a smile of her own.

The two girls sat across from each other on their beds and chatted about where they were from, their interests, and how nervous they were to be freshmen at Princeton. Michelle thought they could probably become good friends; they seemed to have a lot in common. Perhaps Catherine thought the same thing, but the two girls never got a chance to find out.

"She's *black*?" Catherine's mother said to her daughter in horror when they spoke on the phone later that day. "No way. There is no way you're living with a black roommate."

"But I like her," Catherine said.

"That doesn't matter. You have to move."

Catherine's mother immediately called the housing office and demanded that her daughter be switched to a dorm room with a white roommate, claiming, "We're not used to living with black people." Michelle would not know until years later why Catherine had moved out, because Catherine was too embarrassed to tell her at the time.

"Michelle was one of the funniest people I had ever met," Catherine recalled in 2008. "Having to move out was my secret shame."

But there were plenty of other white students at Princeton who were neither ashamed nor secretive about their racism. Michelle found out quickly that she was not particularly welcome in any of the university's "eating clubs." These were social clubs, very much like fraternities and sororities. The club members ate meals together at the club houses, socialized, and threw parties. Many freshmen considered joining an eating club to be a big deal and absolutely necessary, but not everyone was accepted into a club. The clubs chose their new members through interviews and sometimes humiliating contests. At the time

Michelle was at Princeton, most of these clubs were not interested in including minorities.

Michelle, in turn, did not express any interest in being part of one of these clubs. Instead of worrying about where she was not accepted, she sought out other clubs and organizations that were glad to include her. In particular, Michelle spent time volunteering at the school's "Third World Center," an organization specifically for minority students. Here, Michelle found friends from backgrounds far different from that of the typical wealthy, white Princeton student. To her, this experience was much more valuable than the experience of being part of an elite eating club might have been.

"We created a community within a community," Michelle would later say of her experience with the center.

As the years went on at Princeton, Michelle found the Third World Center to be more and more valuable to her. She attended discussion groups that sometimes featured famous civil rights activists. At one such talk, Michelle even got to meet Rosa Parks, the black woman who, in 1955, refused to give up her seat on a bus to a white person. Members of the center also went into the town of Princeton, hoping to bridge the divide between the residents and the university. Many Princeton residents were black, and it was rare for university students to reach out to the townspeople. Michelle was happy to be among one of the first groups of students to do this.

Michelle also had a job at the center. She was in charge of an after-school program for the children of Princeton's maintenance employees. Michelle was a natural with children, and many of the children Michelle looked after developed a bond with her that they would remember all of their lives.

"She was like a big sister to everyone," remembers the son of a janitor. "All the kids loved her. She'd play the 'Charlie Brown' song on the piano, tell jokes, and laugh right along with us. You could tell she liked making us happy."

But perhaps most importantly, the Third World Center gave Michelle a place to talk to other minority students about what it felt like to be black on a nearly all-white campus. Michelle was certainly not alone in feeling that some white students were unfriendly or even downright rude simply because of her skin color.

"It was the first time that I was made very aware that I was black," said one of Michelle's close college friends. "I'd say 'hi' to people, and they would ignore me. Sometimes, people would make racist jokes and then turn to me and say, 'No offense. I don't mean you.' But of course it was offensive, and how could it not mean me?"

Another friend noted that she could not count the number of times white male students referred to her as "Brown Sugar."

"Like Michelle, it was my first experience with that kind of prejudice," she recalled. "And I'd often get asked what my SAT scores were, because they could not believe I was actually smart enough to get into Princeton."

Like her father, Michelle did not waste time or energy complaining when things were hard. Instead, she focused on her classes. In spite of some of her negative experiences, Michelle knew that Princeton was an excellent school. And she knew that the education she was receiving was far more worthy of her attention than were the students who gave her a hard time. Even so, the racism that Michelle experienced at Princeton made an impression on her. The comments, the looks, the unfriendliness; all of this was like a constant unpleasant hum in the back of her mind.

In her final year at Princeton, Michelle wrote her senior paper about her experience as a black student. Titled, "Princeton-Educated Blacks and the Black Community," the paper expressed Michelle's feelings about being black at an Ivy League university.

"I have found that at Princeton, no matter how liberal and open-minded some of my white professors and classmates try to be toward me, I sometimes feel like a visitor on campus, as if I really don't belong," Michelle wrote. "Regardless of the circumstances under which I interact with whites at Princeton, it often seems as if, to them, I will always be black first and a student second."

Michelle was a 21-year-old describing as best she could how it felt to be, at times, on the outside looking in at a famous university. Her professor thought the paper was excellent. In fact, Michelle's paper received a $50 prize from the African American studies program in addition to an A-plus. Little did Michelle know that, decades later, that paper would reappear on the internet while her husband was running for president in 2008.

"This is proof that Michelle Obama hates white people!" some people, who did not want Barack Obama to win, promptly said. "She's trying to divide blacks and whites!"

Such claims were an undeserved attack on Michelle. Not only was this simply a young woman's college project, written many years earlier; there was nothing in it that even hinted that Michelle was racist. She was expressing how she felt others saw *her*, not how she saw others.

"One of the points I was making," Michelle said in 2008, "is that it was a very isolating experience. . . . Different people handle that in different ways."

In fact, Michelle had interviewed numerous other black Princeton students as she did research for her paper. As a sociology major, Michelle studied the behavior of people in different situations. Her paper was simply a study of how being a minority at an Ivy League school affected her and other black students.

In addition to calling Michelle racist, some people used her old paper as "proof" that Michelle hated Princeton. They called her "ungrateful" and "spoiled," despite plenty of evidence to the contrary. Although Michelle's experience at Princeton was not perfect, it was in general a good one. She made many close friends in her dorm who "sat around on the floor on pillows because we couldn't afford any furniture," remembered one friend. "We listened to Stevie Wonder records, talked, giggled, and laughed hysterically."

Michelle was also glad to be at the same college as her big brother. Craig had become a basketball star at Princeton. He was Player of the Year two years in a row. Michelle enjoyed watching her brother play, and Craig even introduced Michelle to some of his friends and teammates who were interested in her. However, Michelle didn't have a serious boyfriend during college.

"Because of the example set by our father, Michelle's expectations for men were very high," Craig later explained. "Very few of my sister's boyfriends ever made it to the meet-the-family stage."

And because she was truly interested in sociology, Michelle did well in her classes. She found many of her professors at Princeton to be motivating and encouraging, and she was excited by the fact that Princeton challenged her at every turn. Michelle accepted every challenge that came along. By the end of her senior year in 1985, she had done so well that she graduated with honors.

But what now?

Many of Michelle's graduating classmates were doing one of two things with their impressive Princeton degrees: interviewing with banks and corporations or applying to law school. Michelle didn't have any interest in working in a bank or in finance. What she really wanted to do was work with people. From a young age, she had been drawn to the idea of helping others and, hopefully, making the world a better place. After a lot of thought, Michelle was leaning toward law school. After all, a lawyer could make things better by fighting for people who had been treated unfairly.

"This was a generation that all read *To Kill a Mockingbird*," said one of Michelle's advisors at Princeton, referring to the famous book by Harper Lee. In the book, a lawyer named Atticus Finch defends a wrongly accused black man in a small town in Alabama in the 1930s. In spite of the racism and threats of the townspeople, the lawyer stands up for what is right.

Michelle thought that maybe she could be that kind of lawyer. And once she had made her decision to become a lawyer, Michelle had to choose a law school.

"I was raised to believe I could do it all," Michelle said in an interview many years later. "And that was very empowering."

With that kind of confidence, Michelle decided that she wouldn't go to just any law school; she would go to the best law school in the United States. Again, she was told that it would be too difficult to get in, that she should really look elsewhere.

"I was a black girl brought up on the South Side of Chicago," Michelle later said. "Was I supposed to go to Princeton? No. Again, they said that Harvard Law School was too much for me to reach for. But guess what? I reached it."

Chapter 5

"*I*f I could do this over, I'm not sure I would."

A confused and disappointed Michelle had called her former boss at the Third World Center, Czerny Brasuell, to talk about life at Harvard.

After a semester in law school, Michelle was doubtful that she had chosen the right path. Brasuell, who had known Michelle well and thought highly of her, had tried to get Michelle to reconsider becoming a lawyer.

"It had nothing to do with her ability," Brasuell later said. "It had to do with understanding what the process of becoming a lawyer was like. There is a big gap between what you see on television or read about. I was pretty certain Michelle would see what I was talking about. And she did—I got the phone call where she talked about the things she didn't like."

Going into law school, Michelle thought she was doing the right thing. After all, with a degree from Princeton and another from Harvard Law

School, the opportunity to be offered excellent high-paying jobs was almost certain. And Michelle needed to earn money; she had taken out some seriously steep loans to pay for college. Michelle, in many ways, was simply doing what she saw her fellow Princeton classmates doing. She was caught up in what she called the "surprisingly narrow" choices that she felt she was supposed to choose from.

"You can be a lawyer or you can work on Wall Street; those are the usual options," Michelle later said. "They're easy, socially acceptable, and financially rewarding. Why wouldn't you do it?"

But in the back of Michelle's mind, she wondered if she should have thought more about her choices. Maybe, she thought, she should have taken a year off between Princeton and Harvard to consider her future. And yet, here she was at *the* best law school. It had not been easy getting accepted (she had been placed on a waiting list), and Michelle knew she was being given a chance that very few young people got, particularly young black women. Only twenty years earlier, barely one percent of Harvard's law students were black. Of those, only a few were women. These were facts that Michelle did not take lightly.

"There was a real sense among the black students at Harvard of the old saying, 'From those to whom much is given, much is expected,'" one of Michelle's Harvard friends pointed out.

And, as always, Michelle expected a great deal from herself. As she would often do throughout her life, she thought of her father's example.

"The lens of life, how I see the world, is through my background, my upbringing," Michelle would later explain.

She would continue to work hard, focus, and not complain. She had made her choice.

Czerny Brasuell knew that Michelle would move forward in spite of the doubts she had expressed during their phone conversation. "I have to say that in addition to things I would place high in a list about Michelle—the loyalty, the respect for people's humanity—she is not a quitter," Brasuell recalled. "She was going to see how this choice would allow her to make certain kinds of things happen in her life."

At law schools, the competition between students is typically intense. Class discussions can quickly turn heated and even insulting. But during arguments in law classes, Michelle was one of the quieter students. She worked hard and made good grades, but showing off and one-upping was not her style.

"She supported other students, but she was never out front," one classmate recalled. "My impression was that she had very strongly held beliefs that she mainly kept to herself unless it was necessary—like when she just couldn't stand it anymore and had to say something."

During her three years at Harvard Law School, Michelle's most rewarding experiences did not happen in the classroom. In the oldest building on campus was a student-run organization called the Legal Aid Office. This is where Michelle felt most involved. The Legal Aid Office helped people who couldn't afford to pay a lawyer. Many of the people who came to the Legal Aid Office had fairly simple problems: conflicts with a landlord, problems collecting money, or questions about divorce. Agreeing to work twenty hours a week in the office, law students gave advice for free.

To Michelle, this job just felt right. She always longed to give back in some way, to help those less fortunate than herself. At Harvard, as it had been at Princeton, she was surrounded by many students who had lots of money and were mostly focused on making a lot more money. Michelle was certainly not *against* making money. But her desire to do something meaningful with her education and her life was stronger than her desire for a high income.

"You can make a lot of money and have a nice degree," Michelle would later comment. "But what are you learning about giving back to the world, and finding your passion and letting *that* guide you?"

After three years of hard work, Michelle graduated on a rainy spring day in 1988. She sat and listened to Harvard's president as he pointed out that barely two percent of Harvard's law graduates would go into careers like legal aid. Nearly all graduates would enter corporate law, where the big money was. He suggested that perhaps more graduates should consider careers that gave back.

Michelle wasn't sure what to do. The summer before her final year at Harvard, she had worked at Sidley and Austin, a corporate law firm in Chicago. The summer job was a sort of test; if she did well, the firm would offer her a job when she graduated. Michelle had already received word from the firm—they wanted to hire her. Her starting salary at age 24 would be $65,000!

Michelle looked over at her parents during the graduation ceremony and smiled at the super-proud expression on her father's face. He was now in a wheelchair, but he continued to work. Even after nearly thirty years working for the city, Fraser Robinson was earning barely half of what his daughter would be paid right out of college. If Michelle felt awkward about this, her parents knew the best way to handle it: through humor.

"We're so proud of you," Marian said as she hugged her daughter. Fraser handed Michelle the Harvard yearbook and told her to look in the back. It was a tradition for parents to buy space in the yearbook for messages of proud congratulations for their sons and daughters. Amid all the messages like, "You made it!" and "Congrats on the job at the best firm!" or "We are so proud!" Michelle found the message from her parents: "We knew you would do this fifteen years ago when we could never make you shut up."

Michelle laughed out loud. She thought of that 11-year-old girl riding her bike around Chicago's South Side, talking non-stop, questioning authority, and brimming with confidence. Now she would be coming back home to work in one of the biggest law firms in the city. Michelle reached out and put her arms around both parents. She knew she owed it all to them.

Michelle's bosses at Sidley and Austin were aware that their new young lawyer wanted work that was interesting and meaningful. However, the lawyers right out of law school tended to get the most boring work. Although she was earning big bucks, Michelle quickly found that she was not really enjoying her job. Then one day, one of her bosses came into her office with a videotape.

"Take a look at this," he said. "This is going to be a new television show, and we need someone to work on the copyright and merchandise rights."

Michelle watched the tape with delight. The show featured a big purple dinosaur named Barney, who spread messages of love and learning to young children. Always interested in anything that would benefit kids and make them laugh, Michelle found this new work appealing. Not long after she had started the Barney project, Michelle's boss wondered if she might be interested in another somewhat unusual "project."

"We have a first-year Harvard Law student we'd like to bring in this summer," Michelle was told. "Would you be interested in being his advisor?"

This was the same summer job Michelle had had a year earlier. It was very unusual for the firm to bring in a first-year law student. Michelle suspected this new guy must be some kind of loud-mouthed showoff.

"I assumed he would be nerdy, strange, and off-putting," Michelle recalled.

Even so, advising a summer "tryout" law student interested Michelle, and it was something of a compliment for her boss to ask her to do it. Advising mostly involved showing the new employee around, answering questions, and making him or her feel at ease. Michelle agreed to be the student's advisor.

"What's the student's name?" she asked.

"Barack Obama."

Michelle thought that was a funny-sounding name, but she didn't think much more about this "Barack" person until she heard people around the office talking about him. Apparently he was several years older than most of the Harvard Law students, because he'd taken some time off before law school. Everyone was saying Barack was brilliant, but when Michelle found out that he was black, she was somewhat irritated.

"I figured they were just impressed with any black man with a suit and a job," she later said. Michelle was also annoyed that *she* had been asked to be Barack's advisor. Was she asked only because they were both black?

Some women in the office looked at the picture Barack had sent in with his resumé. They rushed over to Michelle with it.

"Isn't he handsome?"

Michelle glanced at the picture.

"His ears are too big," was her only comment. Michelle later admitted that she was determined to not like this new hotshot intern. "He sounded too good to be true," she told an interviewer. "I had dated a lot of brothers who had this kind of reputation coming in, so I figured he was one of these smooth brothers who could talk straight and impress people. So, when we first met he had this bad sport jacket and a cigarette dangling from his mouth, and I thought, 'Oh, here we go. Here's this good-looking, smooth-talking guy. I've been down this road before.'"

But in spite of her determination to dislike Barack, Michelle found her new advisee to be charming, and she had to admit that he was, in fact, very handsome. Barack, in turn, thought Michelle was beautiful, and he admired her quick sense of humor, direct manner, and obvious intelligence. The two of them clicked right away. Michelle was also impressed when she learned why Barack had taken several years off before entering law school. He had worked as a "community organizer" in some of the poorest neighborhoods in Chicago, trying to help the people there improve their lives.

Barack, like Michelle, had graduated from a top university, Columbia University in New York City. And like Michelle, he had been offered a high-paying job upon graduation. Barack worked at the job for a while, but what he really wanted to do was help less fortunate people. Finally, he accepted a job in Chicago for barely $10,000 a year. As a community organizer, Barack talked with the people who lived in low-income areas— not far from where Michelle grew up. Then, along with the residents of these neighborhoods, Barack would come up with plans to make things better.

"I was motivated by a single, simple, powerful idea—that I might play a small part in building a better America," Barack Obama explained years later when he first ran for president.

In many ways, Barack was everything Michelle admired and respected in a person. He was far less interested in money than he was in helping others. He was smart and confident, but he could poke fun at himself. He was a good listener, and he could almost always make Michelle laugh.

"When I first met him, I fell in deep like," Michelle would later admit.

Barack clearly felt the same way about Michelle. Almost immediately, he began asking if she would go out with him. But in spite of how she felt, Michelle said no again and again.

"I'm going to focus on *me* this summer," Michelle had told her mother. Also, Michelle thought it was wrong to date an employee she was supposed to be advising, and she told Barack so.

"Come on," Barack said, leaning against her desk with a smile. "What advice are you giving me? You're showing me how the copy machine works. You're telling me which restaurants to try. I don't think the firm will consider one date a serious breach of policy."

Michelle shook her head, trying to hide her own smile. "I can't date another employee," she insisted.

"Then I'll quit," Barack said, grinning. "You're my adviser. Tell me who I have to talk to."

At that, Michelle burst out laughing and ordered Barack out of her office.

But Barack, true to his nature, didn't give up. One afternoon after a company picnic, Michelle drove Barack back to his apartment. Across the street was a Baskin-Robbins ice cream shop.

"How about some ice cream?" Barack said. "It's just an ice cream cone. Not a date. Don't worry!"

Michelle agreed.

"So we sat on the curb and ate ice cream in the sticky afternoon heat," Barack later recalled. "I told her about working at a Baskin-Robbins when

I was a teenager and how hard it was to look cool in a brown apron and a cap. She told me that for a span of two or three years as a child, she had refused to eat anything except peanut butter and jelly."

The two of them laughed at each other's stories. Then Michelle told Barack about her family, the little apartment on the South Side, and her father's illness. She told him how she and Craig used to chatter until midnight through the thin partition between their two sides of the living room.

"I'd like to meet your family," Barack said quietly. Then he looked at Michelle for a long moment.

"May I kiss you?" he asked even more quietly.

Michelle smiled.

"Yes."

Chapter 6

"Michelle was falling hard for him," a coworker remembered. "But she was always cool. She was never falling all over him. She always played it cool."

In fact, Michelle tried to keep the fact that she and Barack were dating a secret from everyone at the law firm. That didn't last too long. Everyone around Barack and Michelle could tell by the way they looked at each other that something was going on.

Although Michelle and Barack were attracted to one another because of some of their similarities, they were, perhaps, more attracted by their differences. Barack later wrote in his book *Dreams from My Father* that he was impressed by how fashionably dressed Michelle was. Michelle, on the other hand found Barack's complete lack of concern about his clothes to be oddly charming.

"His wardrobe was really kind of cruddy," Michelle later told a *Washington Post* reporter. "He had five shirts and seven blue suits and a bunch of ties. I had to really tell him to get rid of the white jacket."

And in an office surrounded by coworkers who were often very concerned about their luxury cars, Michelle was touched by Barack's awful automobile. To her, it said much more about this young man than just the fact that he wasn't into fancy cars.

"That car had so much rust that there was a hole in the passenger door," Michelle recalled. "You could see the ground when you were driving by. I thought, 'This brother is not interested in ever making a dime.' I would just have to love him for his values."

Michelle and Barack were also intrigued by each other's very different backgrounds and families. Barack's father, also named Barack, had been a Kenyan student on scholarship at the University of Hawaii. Barack Sr. met Barack's mother, Ann Dunham, a white woman originally from Kansas, at the university. Ann and Barack Sr. were married for only three years, and soon after their divorce Barack Sr. returned to Kenya. Although Barack Sr. visited him once when he was ten, Barack grew up never really knowing a father. And because his mother travelled frequently, Barack was raised mostly by his grandparents in Hawaii.

"I remember thinking, 'He's biracial! He grew up in Hawaii with white grandparents!' and it all seemed so unusual to me," Michelle later commented.

As for Barack, he was drawn to the close-knit

Robinson family, where both parents had always supported their children, where dinner was eaten at the table every night, and where relatives stopped by all the time.

"It was like dropping in on the set of *Leave It to Beaver*," Barack laughed, remembering his visits to the small apartment on the South Side. "There were aunts and uncles and cousins everywhere, stopping by to sit around the kitchen table and eat until they burst. They'd tell wild stories and laugh deep into the night."

Although Barack may have joked a bit about Michelle's family, he was surprised by how much their closeness moved him.

"For someone like me who had barely known his father," Barack said, "the home that Fraser and Marian Robinson had built for themselves and their children stirred a longing for stability and a sense of place that I had not realized was there."

The Robinsons liked Barack immediately, but they felt a little bad for him. They could tell he liked Michelle a great deal, but they suspected that Michelle wouldn't keep him around for long.

"We gave it a month, tops," Craig later said with a laugh. "It was always that way with Michelle's boyfriends. If they did just one thing wrong, she fired them."

But a month later, Michelle called her brother to ask him for a favor. She wanted him to play a game of basketball with Barack.

"My father and I had a theory that you can really tell what somebody's personality is like by playing basketball with him," Craig recalled. "Is he a show-off? Does he lie about fouling? Is he generous with his passes?"

It was no small thing for Barack to agree to play Craig, even if he didn't know that the game was a way of having his personality analyzed. Not only had Craig been a star player at Princeton; he was later drafted by the Philadelphia 76ers. Although Craig had traded a basketball career for a job on Wall Street, he was still an intense player. But Barack passed the test, even if he had a hard time blocking Craig's shots. He played fairly, competitively, and as toughly as he could.

"My sister is one tough girl," Craig said. "I'm older, and I'm still afraid of her! She needs someone as accomplished as she is, but also someone who can stand up to her. So our family was just hoping that she could hang on to this guy, because it was apparent that he could stand up to her."

And Michelle did hang on to Barack.

Late that summer, Barack took Michelle to a neighborhood organizing meeting in a church basement on the South Side. On their way there, Barack talked about why he was getting a law degree from Harvard. In his years of working as a community organizer, he came to realize that there was only so much he could do to make change. Laws and regulations often blocked the path.

"As a lawyer, I'd be better equipped to really help people," Barack explained. "I just want to make a difference in the lives of people who are less fortunate."

Michelle nodded. She felt the same. Her work at the law firm was not exactly fulfilling, but for the time being, it was helping her pay off her huge student loans. To save even more money, she had moved back in with her parents. But to Michelle, living at home was a plus, not a minus. She had missed her parents terribly while at Princeton and Harvard, and now it seemed like a luxury to sit down to dinner again with them every evening. Still, she hoped that some day, in some way, she would also work to better people's lives.

When Michelle and Barack arrived at the community meeting, many of the people there greeted Barack enthusiastically. They gathered around this young man they had come to trust and admire. These were poor people who barely made it from paycheck to paycheck, but they were hopeful that things could change. Michelle could tell that they believed in Barack and knew that his heart was in the work he was doing.

"His talk that evening was about the world as it is and the world as it should be," Michelle recalled. "He connected with me and everyone in that church basement. And right then and there, I decided this guy was special. The authenticity you see is real, and that's why I fell in love with him."

Barack and Michelle were in love, but their relationship had to be long-distance until Barack finished his last two years of law school at Harvard. He returned to Chicago for the summers, becoming a regular dinner guest at the Robinson house. Michelle even traveled to Hawaii with Barack to meet his grandparents. Things were getting pretty serious, and Michelle started bringing up the subject of marriage. Barack, however, kept telling Michelle that marriage didn't really matter. He told her that how they felt about each other was the most important thing. Sometimes Michelle laughed at Barack's response, but other times she argued with him about the importance of marriage.

About two years after Michelle and Barack became involved, Michelle's best friend from Princeton died after a struggle with cancer. She was only 26. In addition to feeling great sorrow, Michelle also felt frustration. She thought how quickly life could end, and began to question the life she was leading at the law firm.

"How would I want to be remembered in life?" Michelle wondered. "Was I waking up every morning feeling excited about work and the work I was doing? The answer to the question was no."

Then, not even a year later, Michelle's father suddenly died. His multiple sclerosis had been getting worse and had created breathing problems. One night, he struggled to breathe, fell into a coma, and never recovered. He had been employed at the water plant until the day he died.

Michelle was heartbroken. Even as a grown woman, she had loved to sit on the sofa curled up next to her father, with her arms around him. Her "rock," her inspiration, the man she had never wanted to disappoint, was gone at only 55. At the funeral, Michelle wept as she leaned against Barack.

"As the casket was lowered, I promised Fraser Robinson that I would take care of his girl," Barack later wrote. "I realized that in some unspoken way, she and I were already becoming a family."

"With divorce rates so high, is marriage even worthwhile?" Barack was needling Michelle again on the topic of marriage. "I just can't believe you would even say that!" Michelle fumed. "Do you really believe that getting married is that worthless?" "Well, it's how we *feel* that is worth the most," Barack countered. "That's ridiculous," Michelle snapped. "I'm not sure I even want to go out to dinner with you tonight."

Barack hid his smile. Sometimes, he liked to bring up this debate just to get Michelle going. He knew that she wanted to marry him. What's more, Barack had always known, almost from the first moment he met Michelle, that she would be the woman he would marry. All along, he had been playing with her when he'd said that marriage "didn't matter."

That evening, Barack took Michelle to one of Chicago's fanciest restaurants. Michelle was enjoying the romantic dinner, resolving not to mention the word "marriage" that evening. Then, out of the blue, Barack started teasing her on the subject. Michelle had had enough. She let Barack know that he'd better get serious about their relationship if he wanted it to continue. She was still lecturing Barack when dessert came. On her dessert plate was an engagement ring. Michelle stopped mid-sentence.

Years later, Michelle recalled that evening with a laugh: "Barack said, 'That kind of shuts you up, doesn't it?' And, you know, I don't even remember what the dessert was. I don't think I even ate it. I was so shocked and kind of embarrassed because he did sort of shut me up."

That next October of 1992, Michelle and Barack were married by Reverend Jeremiah Wright, a minister Barack had met through his community organizing work. For several months, the two of them lived with Michelle's mother in the tiny apartment on Euclid Street. Then they moved into an apartment of their own in an area of Chicago called Hyde Park. By this point, Barack had graduated from Harvard and was working as a civil rights lawyer, focusing on cases that would help the people of Chicago's South Side. Michelle, too, had begun a new job. The loss of her best friend had made her question what she was doing with her life. But the death of her father had pushed her to make a change.

"I had a fancy office, a secretary, and a new Saab, but it wasn't enough," Michelle remembered. "I looked out at the neighborhood where I grew up and sort of had an awakening. I had to bring my skills to bear in the place that had made me." Many of Michelle's friends and coworkers could not believe that she would actually quit her job at Sidley and Austin. She was considered one of the best new lawyers the firm had hired, and her bosses claimed she would be a "superstar" before she was thirty. The money she could make would have been unbelievable. Michelle didn't care. Some things were more important than money. Barack knew that Michelle would likely cut her salary in half if she began working for a charity or took a community service job. He didn't care either. He supported her 100 percent.

Michelle began her job search by sending out letters to organizations where she thought her skills and education could be used to help people. One of her letters caught the attention of a woman named Valerie Jarrett, who worked in the Chicago mayor's office. Valerie called Michelle and to invited her to interview for a job. The job would involve solving problems that businesses and individuals had with City Hall.

Michelle wasn't sure what to say at first. The job sounded interesting, but the mayor, Richard M. Daley, was the son of a past mayor, Richard J. Daley. Richard J. Daley had been mayor when

Michelle was growing up, and she remembered how he had fought to keep black people in their "own" small neighborhoods. He had also worked to keep black children in the poorer schools. It had made Michelle's parents, and now Michelle, distrustful of politicians—particularly those named Daley. Even so, Michelle decided to go to the interview. What harm could it do to talk with Valerie Jarrett?

What was supposed to be a 20-minute interview lasted an hour and a half. Michelle and Valerie hit it off immediately, and Michelle could tell that *this* mayor's office was not like the old Daley office. "She was so confident and committed and extremely open," Valerie recalled of Michelle. "I offered her the job at the end of the interview."

Michelle enjoyed her new job and quickly worked her way up to assistant commissioner of planning and development. About a year and a half later, Barack told Michelle about a phone call he had received from a charity called Public Allies. This was an organization based in Washington, D.C., that trained young people to become community service leaders. Now they wanted to open an office in Chicago, and they had heard about all the good work Barack had done in Chicago communities. They needed a new boss: someone who could run the new office, manage the problems and questions of the young trainees, and also do community service work.

"They asked me if I wanted the job," Barack told Michelle.

"Well, what did you say?" Michelle asked. She doubted Barack would leave his job as a civil rights lawyer, but Public Allies sounded like the exact sort of organization that both of them would love to work with.

Barack grinned. "I told them that the person they really needed to hire was you."

Chapter 7

"*Boy, she's tall!* was my first impression of Michelle Obama," Jacky Grimshaw, who interviewed Michelle for the Public Allies job, recalled. (Michelle is nearly six feet tall.) But soon after that, Grimshaw saw that Michelle also had a warm personality, was clearly smart, and was very personable.

"We had young people who needed guidance, and we needed a young person to be their leader," Grimshaw explained. "Michelle seemed like a perfect fit."

A big part of the job would involve going into rough neighborhoods with the trainees and helping them interact with all kinds of people, possibly even dangerous people. Would Michelle, a 29-year-old woman, be comfortable doing this kind of work?

"It sounded risky and just kind of out there," Michelle remembered. "But for some reason it just spoke to me. This was the first time I said, 'This is what I say I care about. Right here. And I will have to do this.'"

As with her job at City Hall, Michelle was offered the job right away. She was thrilled to accept it in spite of the fact that she would now be making even less money than she had working for the mayor's office. The national director for Public Allies was truly surprised that they were able to hire Michelle.

"She had a law degree from Harvard and had worked for a corporate law firm," he said. "In comparison, I had worked with a telemarketing group!"

Right away, Michelle proved to be a thoughtful but tough boss. She had to deal with one trainee who got so angry during a meeting that he punched a hole in the wall. Another drank a fair amount of vodka before coming to work one morning because he was having troubles at home.

"I hear that," Michelle had said, firmly but kindly, to the drunk trainee. "But that can't be how you're defining your choice for the morning. This is about *you*. Let's talk about how we can work this out."

Michelle was at ease working with trainees at some of Chicago's most crime-filled housing projects. And she never felt intimidated when sitting down with the mayor's chief of staff to discuss Public Allies' plans to help people in poor neighborhoods.

"She always had a really amazing combination of unruffled calm and extreme clarity about what needed to happen next," one coworker said of Michelle. "You had to respect her, even if you were mad at her."

Michelle worked at Public Allies for four years. She made so much progress for the organization in Chicago that the national director credited Michelle for building it from the ground up.

"And she built it to last," he said.

Both Barack and Michelle were in jobs that were meaningful. They were working hard to help others, and they enjoyed their work. But still, the question nagged at them: *Could I be doing more?* In 1995, both of the Obamas were feeling restless. Michelle moved to a position at the University of Chicago. Her job there was to encourage college students to volunteer in the poor South Side neighborhoods that backed up to the university. An institution as big as a university gave Michelle more opportunities to reach out and make a difference. In addition, it was a huge step for the University of Chicago to even consider the welfare of their South Side neighbors.

"I grew up five minutes from the campus," Michelle recalled. "All the buildings have their back to the community. The university didn't think kids like me existed. And I certainly didn't want to have anything to do with that place."

Now Michelle had the unusual opportunity of being able to turn things around at a large institution. The very place that once pretended that "girls like her" didn't exist was now asking for her help. What's more, she could help bring positive changes to the community where she grew up.

But what about Barack? Michelle could tell that her husband was getting impatient.

Barack had worked three years as a civil rights attorney, focusing mostly on cases that helped the people of Chicago's South Side. This was work he loved, but sometimes this work didn't seem as if it accomplished enough. To do more, Barack also taught a class at the University of Chicago.

And as if that were not enough, Barack also managed to write a book in 1995. *Dreams from My Father* told the story of Barack's unusual childhood and young adult life. It was a wonderful book, but no one knew who Barack Obama was at the time; or, at least, not enough people knew who Barack Obama was to make the book a success. Only nine people showed up at his book signing in downtown Chicago. At the time, it didn't even sell enough copies to earn back the $30,000 advance the publishing company had given to Barack. (However, when the book was reissued years later when Barack ran for president, it would sell several million copies.)

In spite of all this, Barack felt unfulfilled.

Barack had become a lawyer so that he could help make changes. But now, he saw changes that needed to be made that required something more than a lawyer. Lawyers work to make sure the laws in place help and protect people. But, Barack realized, it was *politicians* who created the bills that would, hopefully, turn into new and better laws.

Barack had never kept his interest in politics a secret from his wife. Nor had Michelle ever hidden her dislike of politics from her husband. Certainly, there were some politicians Michelle respected, but having grown up during a politically messy time in Chicago, she was cautious.

"I, like most people, have been very reluctant about politics," Michelle later explained. "Politics is a nasty business, and you don't hold out hope that fairness will win. It's like a business. So, there was that part of me that said 'Do Barack and I want to put ourselves out for a system that I am not sure about?'"

In addition, Barack was now 34, and Michelle was 31. Michelle was ready to start a family. If Barack won the Illinois State Senate seat that he was interested in, he would be working three hours away from Chicago at the state capital in Springfield, Illinois. How much would Barack be away from home and from the children the two of them hoped to be raising soon? Michelle was also less than thrilled with how public much of her life would have to be if Barack became a senator.

"I'm pretty private," she stated in an interview. "I like to surround myself with people that I trust and love."

And that did not include many politicians.

Still, Michelle believed that if anyone could make a difference, Barack could. Perhaps if he were in office, real and good change might come about. So, when he asked for her blessing for getting involved in politics (something he would always do when it came to running for office), she gave him the go-ahead. In addition, Michelle agreed to help her husband's campaign, often speaking to groups and accompanying him to fundraising events.

Barack had decided to run for the Illinois State Senate when the current state senator, Alice Palmer, decided to leave her position and run for a seat in the United States Congress. Palmer believed in Barack and agreed with his views, so she was happy to support him. Then, everything changed. After campaigning for a few months, Palmer realized that she had no chance of winning her run for Congress. She decided she wanted her old state senate position back.

Barack said no. His campaigning was going well, and it looked like he would win. Some people in Illinois were angry with Barack for refusing to step down. They pointed out that he was young and would have many opportunities to run for office, while Palmer, who was much older, would not. However, Barack was both competitive and eager to start his political career. In fact, he was so involved with the campaign that he was not with his mother when she died in November 1995, of ovarian cancer. To this day, Barack says that not being by his mother's side at that moment is his life's biggest regret.

"I want to do everything and be everything," he once said. "And that can sometimes get me into trouble."

When Barack won the state senate position, he wasn't very warmly welcomed by the other senators. Some thought he was too young and overly ambitious. Others thought he was too proud of his fancy law degree and the fact that he was a published author. Still others were simply jealous; Barack was energetic, positive, and good-looking. Voters from all different backgrounds liked him, a rare achievement that other politicians envied.

In spite of the chilly welcome, Barack got to work right away. One of the things that had frustrated Barack in his work as a lawyer was that he couldn't change the law; he could only follow it. However, now, as a state senator, he was a lawmaker. In Barack's first two terms, he got a total of twenty-eight laws passed. No longer did the other senators question his ability or ambition. Barack Obama was on his way.

But while Barack was growing more and more well-known, Michelle was growing more and more frustrated.

"Being a political wife is not easy," one friend commented. "Your ego is stomped on, and you're often pushed aside. You're the senator's wife . . .

you're never a person in your own being. It's very, very hard on the family."

And it was.

In 1998, Michelle gave birth to the Obamas' first daughter, Malia. When they got married, Barack and Michelle had agreed that their children would have the same kind of childhood Michelle had had: dinner together with the family every night. But now Barack was in Springfield four out of seven days a week; dinner together was rare. Michelle was still working full time and trying to take care of a baby mostly on her own. She and Barack began arguing more and more. And when Barack expressed his desire to run for the United States Congress in 2000, Michelle nearly blew up.

"My wife's anger toward me seemed barely contained," Barack later wrote about that time. "'You only think about yourself,' she would tell me. 'I never thought I'd have to raise a family alone!'"

Barack lost the race for Congress, but his busy schedule did not slow down. In the summer of 2001, the Obamas' second daughter, Natasha (whom they call Sasha) was born. Now Michelle had twice as much work. On a family vacation to Hawaii, she was so angry with her husband that she would barely speak to him. Something had to give. In spite of her anger, Michelle knew how very deeply Barack loved both her and his two daughters. And she admired his dedication to making changes in the lives of less fortunate people. Barack was working so hard that sometimes he was exhausted. In spite of that, he tried to spend as much time and energy as he possibly could with his family. Michelle decided to give Barack a break.

"I spent a lot of time expecting my husband to fix things," Michelle later said. "But then I realized he was there in the ways he could be. If he wasn't there, it didn't mean he wasn't a good father or didn't care."

Michelle, like her husband, had often been determined to "do it all," but when she finally asked her mother to help with the two girls—something Marian was very happy to do—life got much easier.

"Once I was okay with that, my marriage got better," Michelle said. She also figured out how to mesh her schedule with Barack's. Michelle liked to go to sleep early, but her husband often stayed up until two in the morning working, writing, or watching sports. Instead of waking up at five a.m. and being angry that Barack was sound asleep, she wedged in her workout at the gym. Often, she was already stretching and doing sit-ups at 4:30 a.m. By the time she got home, Barack was fixing breakfast for the two girls.

Michelle didn't mention it very often, but when Barack had lost the race for Congress, she had hoped that once his state senate term was over, he might quit politics for good. She often thought that the people who surrounded Barack in political circles were phony and friendly toward her husband only to gain power or favors. She hoped he might return to his civil rights law work.

But Barack had other plans. At first, his political loss stung, and he went through a period of sadness. However, as always, Barack Obama was no quitter. He thought about what he might have done wrong and how he could fix things in the next campaign. But did he want a "next campaign"? Barack was still a young man, and he knew that he had many years in which he could work for change in America. Still, there was no time like the present.

"I think I want to be a senator," Barack said carefully to Michelle one afternoon in 2003.

Michelle gave her husband a funny look. "You're already a senator."

"I mean a senator in the United States Senate."

Michelle wasn't sure how to feel. There had been only four black senators in the entire history of the United States Senate. Michelle knew if Barack won, it would mean a great deal to African Americans. And beyond that, she truly believed that Barack would be a great senator. She knew by now that Barack did indeed make change happen whenever he had the opportunity.

"If I lose, I promise that will be the end of politics," Barack added.

Michelle still wasn't sure. How on earth were they going to pay for another campaign? They still had student loans to pay off, and now they had two young girls as well. Even Barack's credit card was maxed out.

"Look. Here's what's going to happen," Barack promised Michelle. "I'm going to win the primary, win that general election, and then I'm going to write another book to help with the expenses."

Another book?

Years later, Michelle would recall what she thought when Barack first said that. "I was thinking, 'Just write a book, yeah, that's right. Yep, yep, yep. And you'll climb the beanstalk and come back down with the golden egg, Jack.'"

But Michelle didn't say that. She looked at her husband. He seemed so confident, so ready to succeed this time. He had good reason. His seven years in the state legislature had created an excellent reputation for him. The people of Illinois definitely knew him now, and they liked him—a lot.

"All right," Michelle finally said. Then, covering her smile, she added, "But don't count on *my* vote."

Chapter 8

"*T*he typical response to person of color in these small towns," an Illinois magazine reporter bluntly wrote, "is to roll up the car windows."

Many reporters and political experts figured that white blue-collar voters in the small towns of southern Illinois would not support a young African American candidate. They also didn't think Barack Obama could possibly raise enough campaign money to keep going.

Barack and Michelle didn't listen to all the so-called experts. Michelle knew Barack would do what he had always done with small-town people who would supposedly not vote for him just because of his skin color: he would meet the people and listen to *them*. For months, he traveled all over Illinois, meeting people in the cities, towns, and crossroads. He wanted to know what they were concerned about, what troubled them, what gave them hope.

"Barack's got something different," a white factory worker in a small southern Illinois town told reporters. "He makes you feel like he's not a politician, but a leader."

While Barack's opponent ran a negative campaign, Barack ran a positive campaign. It was during this time that the campaign slogan, "Yes We Can!" was created. At first, Obama didn't like it, thinking the wording was too simple. Michelle, however, saw right away that the slogan had power. Voters wanted an optimistic, direct approach. Michelle understood that they wanted to believe that yes, they could be a part of making change happen. Many politicians had failed to realize one very important fact: Americans want to feel involved in our political system. They don't want to just sit back and watch the politicians make all the decisions.

However, in spite of Barack's ability to connect with voters and his good reputation in his district, many voters in Illinois still didn't really know who he was. Barack and his campaign manager, David Axelrod, worked hard, but Barack still needed some kind of breakthrough to guarantee his election to the United States Senate.

Then, in the summer of 2003, that break-through appeared. One morning, an important phone call came in. John Kerry, the Democratic nominee for President of the United States, had a question: Would Barack Obama be interested in presenting the keynote speech at the Democratic National Convention the following summer? Kerry believed that Barack best represented the future of the Democratic Party. He was young and energetic, with a positive, welcoming attitude.

Barack didn't need even five minutes to think about this opportunity. The keynote at the convention was one of the most important speeches. It set the tone for the campaign, and it was considered a huge honor to be asked to be the keynote speaker. Barack immediately said yes. The convention would put him on a national stage just three months before Election Day. Not only would millions of Illinois voters be watching; many more millions of Americans everywhere would be watching!

The night of the speech, Michelle waited backstage with Barack, some friends and campaign workers, and her brother, Craig. Craig was pacing back and forth and sweating. He looked at Michelle wonderingly. What advice would she give her husband? Only a few years earlier, Craig had called his younger sister for advice. He wasn't enjoying his work in the financial world, in spite of all the money he was earning.

"Well, what would you really like to do?" Michelle had asked.

"Coach college basketball," Craig had replied.

"Brother, you've gotta follow your heart," Michelle said. "Go for it."

He was now coaching, earning barely ten percent of what he had been earning before, and he was happier than ever. Little sister had had some awesome advice. Now, only moments before Barack walked out on stage, Michelle reached over to straighten his tie. She could tell he was nervous. What words of wisdom could she give her husband at a moment like this?

"Just don't screw it up, buddy!" she said.

Barack laughed out loud. Michelle's humor and timing had been exactly what he needed. Barack relaxed and took a deep breath. Then he walked out into the spotlights, the roar of the crowd, and a speech that would change his and Michelle's lives forever.

"Tonight is a particular honor for me because, let's face it, my presence on this stage is pretty unlikely."

Thus, Barack Obama began the keynote address at the 2004 Democratic National Convention.

"There's not a liberal America and a conservative America—there's a *United States* of America. There's not a black America and a white America and a Latino America and an Asian America—there's the *United States* of America. . . . We are one people. . . ."

At first, many in the crowd wondered who this tall, thin man with the funny name was. But as Barack told the story of his unusual background and how, because of the freedoms and the greatness of our country, he was able to make his hopes and dreams come true, the crowd became electrified. Obama was a dynamic and sincere speaker. No one had ever seen a politician quite like him before.

"In the end, that is God's greatest gift to us, the bedrock of this nation; the belief in things not seen; the belief that there are better days ahead. . . . I believe that as we stand on the crossroads of history, we can make the right choices, and meet the challenges that face us."

When Obama finished his speech that evening, the entire convention erupted. Many people had tears streaming down their faces, while others could not stop grinning. Writers and reporters rushed to write about this amazing young politician. Within hours of Obama's speech, many were calling it one of the greatest speeches in recent history. Suddenly, the entire nation knew who Barack Obama was— and now they wanted to know more.

"It's like walking around with Michael Jordan now," Craig said in the days following the speech. "It really is. My sister and Barack are suddenly famous!"

Three months later, Barack won the senate race by a landslide. And then, because of his newfound fame, Barack was able to follow through on his promise to Michelle. He was asked by a publisher to write not one book, but *three* books: another book about his life and two children's books to be co-authored with Michelle. The advance for the three books was $1.9 million. In addition, his *Dreams from My Father* was now bound for the bestseller list. Not only was Obama able to pay off his credit cards and student loans; he also paid cash for a beautiful new home for his family.

As Michelle and Barack flew to Washington, D.C., in January of 2005 for Barack's swearing in as the freshman senator from Illinois, Michelle remembered the promises her husband had made before beginning the Senate race.

"I can't believe you pulled it off," she said with a smile and a kiss on his cheek.

"Daddy, are you going to be president?"

Six-year-old Malia looked up at her father questioningly. Barack looked around at the press and photographers who had gathered to interview Barack after the swearing-in ceremony for new senators. He smiled in an embarrassed way and looked at Michelle. Michelle just smiled back with a look that said, *Of course you're not.*

"Well, Senator, *are* you?" a reporter from the *Chicago Tribune* pressed.

In spite of his private ambitions, Barack knew better than to say *Yes* or even *Maybe*. Years earlier, when Michelle had first introduced Barack to her family, Craig had asked Michelle's new boyfriend what he planned to do after law school.

"I'd like to teach," Barack said. "Or maybe run for office."

"You mean like City Council or something?"

"No," Barack said. "Like the Senate. Maybe even president."

"President of what?" Craig asked with a funny look.

"The United States."

"Whoa," Craig had said, looking around the room full of Robinson relatives and lowering his voice. "Come on over and meet my aunt, but don't tell her *that*!"

Barack's campaign manager handled the growing questions about whether or not Senator Obama was considering a run for the presidency in 2008. He responded by saying there were no plans for a campaign. When Barack was asked directly, he often simply said, "I was just elected senator! I am not going to run for president in 2008." Michelle assumed this was true.

But the seed had been planted in Barack's mind. Still, he had to focus on his new job as a senator first.

After much discussion and consideration, Michelle and Barack decided it would be best for Michelle, Malia, and Sasha to stay in Chicago instead of moving to Washington, D.C. Some people thought Michelle was making a mistake not accompanying her husband to Washington, but Michelle did not want to be just a "senator's wife." She had her daughters' lives to think about and her own career in Chicago.

Others casually mentioned how many women might be after Barack, a young and handsome senator.

"I can't worry about some other woman pushing up against my husband," Michelle bluntly said to a reporter. "If somebody can come between us, we didn't have much to begin with."

Barack was even more direct when asked what he thought about all the female chatter about him (including the viral YouTube music video "I've Got a Crush on Obama"). Would he ever cheat on Michelle?

"Michelle would kick my butt," Barack said. "Not only would it not be worth it, but I seriously would not want to have to deal with *that*."

In reality, many families of senators did not live in Washington. Barack rented an apartment in Washington and stayed there Monday through Thursday, and then he flew home on Friday afternoons. Sometimes it was lonely for Barack, and he missed his two young daughters terribly. Still, his time in Washington gave Barack the time and focus he needed to learn the ropes of being a senator.

"It's like trying to drink from a fire hose," Barack later wrote about the experience of being new to Congress. There was so much information to learn, so many people asking for his time, so many demands, that Barack had to be careful not to get overwhelmed. But he was an impressive young senator. He spoke out against the war in Iraq. He worked to pass laws that would limit nuclear weapons in Russia and other countries.

And after Hurricane Katrina devastated much of New Orleans, Barack slammed the slow response of the U.S. government to help the victims.

Nationwide, this new senator from Illinois was turning heads. When he spoke, people listened. Even Republicans were admitting that if Obama made a run for the presidency in 2008, he would be tough competition.

By 2006, both Barack and Michelle had reached near rock-star status. Everyone loved seeing them interviewed, particularly together. Their sense of humor and obvious admiration and love for one another made them talk-show favorites. On *Oprah*, Barack explained how he had tried to become more involved in his girls' birthday parties, even offering to get goody bags—until Michelle had told him he would have to go to a party store, pick out assorted favors, and have both boys' and girls' bags.

"You'd walk into that party store, and your head would explode," Michelle said to an outburst of audience laughter. Then as the laughter died down, Oprah got right to the point.

"So, *are* you going to run for president?" she asked Barack.

Barack wouldn't answer the question with a yes or a no, but the pressure was getting stronger. Finally, in late 2006, Obama told a news reporter, "I have thought about it," but later indicated that it was up to Michelle. Michelle thought long and hard about it. She and Barack discussed a run for the presidency at length. Understandably, Michelle worried about her husband's safety and the effect a national campaign and then the presidency might have on their young daughters.

"Honestly, the last thing I wanted for my girls was to have them grow up in this and have their lives turned upside down," Michelle later said. "I didn't want to have them hear their parents being criticized on national TV."

Michelle also wondered about the direction of her own life. Would she be okay with leaving her career? She wasn't sure that being First Lady was something she'd want to do or even be good at.

"I took myself down every dark road you could go on, just to prepare myself before we jumped out there," Michelle said in an interview. "Eventually I thought, 'This is a smart man with a good heart, and if the only reason I wouldn't want him to be president is that I'm married to him, I can't be that selfish.'"

Michelle was ready to give her blessing once again. But there was one little detail she insisted upon first. Michelle asked her husband to make a promise.

"I asked him to quit smoking. For good," Michelle revealed to the press. "The president should not smoke, you know?"

Also, Michelle and Barack both agreed that he should not be doing something that both of them had already told their girls *they* should not do. Barack had tried kicking the habit for years, but now he threw out his cigarettes and gave Michelle (and Malia and Sasha) the promise. In return, she gave him the go-ahead.

The evening after Barack announced his candidacy, he and Michelle sat down with their daughters to try to explain what would be happening over the next year or more. Finally, in answer to Malia's question of two years earlier, Barack told his daughter that, yes, he was going to at least *try* to become president. Malia, however, was two years older and two years wiser.

"So, you're going to try to be president?" Malia asked, unimpressed. "Shouldn't you be vice president first?"

Chapter 9

"*O*ur lives are close to normal, if there is such a thing when you're running for president," Michelle said in an interview during the presidential campaign in 2007. "When I'm off the road, I'm going to Target to get toilet paper or something, I'm standing on soccer fields, but I think there's just a level of connection that gets lost the further you get into being a candidate."

Michelle worked very hard to maintain that "level of connection" to normal life with her daughters. She had agreed to help with fundraising, give speeches, and accompany Barack when she could. But Michelle put some strict rules in place. If the girls had any important events like soccer games or ballet recitals after school, Michelle stayed in Chicago. Otherwise, she flew out in the morning to wherever she was needed, insisting on being home before the girls went to bed.

"Yeah, I'm a little tired at the end of the day," she said in an interview. "But the girls, they just think Mommy was at work. They don't know I was in New Hampshire. Quite frankly, they don't care."

Michelle and Barack had promised their daughters that they would get a puppy when the campaign was over. Michelle often joked that Malia and Sasha were far more concerned about the prospect of getting a dog than the prospect of their father becoming president.

At the start of the campaign, Marian Robinson, who was still living in the small apartment on the South Side, retired from the secretarial job she had taken after Fraser died. Now she was able to spend more time taking care of her grandchildren.

"Thank God for Grandma!" Michelle said to crowds nationwide during her speeches.

Michelle was a remarkably skilled speaker who was good at telling people why they should vote for Barack. Many reporters commented that she was often more convincing than Barack himself! Michelle had a natural and warm speaking style that pulled listeners in. In addition, she was smart and often quite funny.

"I want to introduce the Obamas the *people*, not the Obamas the resumés," she explained. She wasn't interested in rattling off a list of her and Barack's achievements. She knew people would relate more to hearing about Barack's unusual childhood or about her remarkable father. Crowds would be touched more by what Barack's hopeful vision was for this country, not by how well he had done at Harvard. Michelle also loved telling funny stories about Barack and poking fun at him.

"This Barack Obama guy's pretty impressive," she told a crowd in New York. "Then"—she paused and raised her eyebrows—"there's the Barack Obama that lives in my house."

The crowd laughed and clapped.

"That guy's not as impressive," Michelle continued. "He still has trouble putting the bread up and putting his socks actually in the dirty clothes. And he still doesn't do a better job than our five-year-old daughter, Sasha, making his bed. So you have to forgive me if I'm a little stunned by this whole Barack Obama thing."

Crowds loved it. Michelle could not be happier than when she could feel that connection and know that she was helping Americans get to know Barack, even if it was just through funny stories. The more they knew him, the more likely they might be to vote for him in the primary, the race to see who the Democratic Party's nominee for president would be. If he won the primary, these same voters would support him in the race for president. And, of course, Michelle captured the hearts and the attention of the crowds with more than funny stories about her husband and herself. She spoke of their dreams, their children, their vision for a better and more hopeful America.

"When Barack graduated from college, he didn't go to work on Wall Street and make a lot of money," Michelle told a crowd in New Hampshire. "He became a community organizer, working in some of the toughest neighborhoods on the South Side of Chicago, with folks who had reason to be cynical, because the government had forgotten a lot of folks who lived in these neighborhoods. . . . We need a different leadership. We need a Barack Obama presidency!"

As the weeks went by, Michelle was surprised at how much she actually enjoyed campaigning. But there were downsides to working Barack's campaign, too. For one thing, as always, Michelle was simply not a big fan of politics.

"The game of politics is the thing I dislike the most about this whole process," she told one interviewer. "It's rough and tumble."

And fundraising was not exactly enjoyable for Michelle either. Michelle knew that a successful presidential campaign could not be run without millions of dollars, and that money had to be raised. But asking for money was not her style. When asked by a *Newsweek* reporter how she felt about it, Michelle did not mince words.

"I hate fundraising. Haaaaaaate it. Hate, *hate* it."

And as the campaign went on, both Michelle and Barack were the targets of verbal attacks, lies, and outright hatred. Some Americans disliked the idea of an African American president, and they used their own racism to try to claim that Michelle was a racist. It was during this time that someone dug up Michelle's old senior paper from Princeton and used it to try to prove she hated white people.

Then a rumor circulated nationwide that there was a recording of Michelle referring to Caucasian people as "whitey."

Michelle practically laughed out loud over this ridiculous lie.

"Seriously?" she said to an interviewer. "I mean, '*whitey*'? That's something that George Jefferson [a 1970s sitcom character] would say. Anyone who says that doesn't know me. They don't know the life I've lived. They don't know anything about me."

The name-calling, accusations, and outrageous lies trailed after the Obamas like a cloud of pollution. One conspiracy group even attempted to convince voters that Michelle was actually a *man* named Michael! And after Michelle gave Barack an affectionate fist bump following a speech, a Fox News commentator claimed that the Obamas were sharing a "terrorist fist jab." Many Americans at the time were not familiar with the harmless gesture and believed the commentator. Not much later, Fox News hit another new low when it referred to Michelle insultingly as "Obama's baby mama."

Michelle took everything in stride, refusing to engage with the haters. Instead, she faced the real fact of racism in the United States head-on, telling voters that a national conversation needed to take place and that things had to change.

"I've heard some folks say that America's not ready for a black president," Michelle said at a rally in Iowa. "We've heard those voices before. . . . Voices that focus on what might go wrong, rather than what's possible. And I understand it. I know where it comes from. It's the bitter legacy of racism and discrimination and oppression in this country. A legacy that hurts us all."

"We are still too divided," Michelle noted in a speech in South Carolina. "We are still a nation that is too cynical. . . . We're mean."

Some Americans didn't like Michelle's honesty and directness, but many found it refreshing. Michelle spoke her mind, but sometimes that got her into trouble. In one interview, she said that "for the first time in my adult life, I am really proud of my country." Her critics jumped on her immediately, claiming that Michelle Obama was not proud of America.

"She hates America!"

"Unpatriotic!"

"Racist!"

Michelle did what she could to set the record straight.

"What I was clearly talking about was that I'm proud of how Americans are engaging in the political process," she told the *Los Angeles Times*. "For the first time in my lifetime, I'm seeing people roll up their sleeves in a way that I haven't seen and really trying to figure this out. That's the source of pride I was talking about."

But that's not what Michelle had originally said. Those who were looking for any reason to attack the Obamas didn't buy it and wouldn't let the comment go. It haunted Michelle for months.

"I knew it was never going to be easy," Michelle said of campaigning and the often-uncomfortable national spotlight. And then, as always, she moved on to the work that remained to be done.

As the Democratic primary race went on, it came down to two candidates: Barack Obama and Hillary Clinton. Barack and Michelle were determined to keep the campaign positive, with no personal attacks on Clinton. But Clinton was not as positive in her approach. She attacked Barack's qualifications, referring to him as inexperienced and clueless about how to get things done. She implied that Barack was all talk and no action or plan, despite his many accomplishments as a senator.

"There's a big difference between us—speeches versus solutions," Clinton told a crowd in 2008.

Some of Barack's advisors told him to fight back harder during debates. They suggested that Michelle should become more aggressive and speak out against Clinton. But the Obamas, for the most part, kept the campaign positive. And a funny thing happened: suddenly Barack was moving ahead in the polls. No one had expected it. Nearly every political analyst had assumed that Clinton, a senator and a former first lady, would quickly overtake Obama. Instead, voters responded more favorably to a message of hope and fairness. Attacks and untrue comparisons seemed only to bring Clinton's numbers down.

And something else was happening too. "There seems to be a youthquake," a *Time* magazine writer observed. "Young people sense that they are coming of age at a time when leadership, and their role in choosing it, *really* matters."

Barack and Michelle Obama drew in young voters like no other presidential candidate and his wife in the history of campaigns. Michelle had always enjoyed interacting with young people, and the connection was instant and real. Also, she was funny, hip, and very stylish. Young women suddenly wanted the same dress or earrings that Michelle had worn at a rally. Barack, too, developed the same kind of connection in his own way. He quickly reached millions of young people through social networking and a broad online presence. No candidate had ever done this before.

Then a music video, featuring celebrities including will.i.am, Jacob Dylan, Scarlett Johansson, Kareem Abdul-Jabbar, Common, John Legend and more singing "Yes We Can," with Barack giving a hope-filled speech in the background, went viral. In 2008, something "going viral" was a fairly new concept. Suddenly young people nationwide were fired up. They headed to the polls for the primaries in record numbers. On August 28, 2008, in Denver, Colorado, only four years after an unknown Barack Obama had given the keynote speech at the Democratic National Convention, he was now the Democratic nominee for President of the United States. This was the first time in our country's history that an African American person had been the nominee of a major party.

A month before the convention, Michelle began practicing the speech she would be giving on the convention's first evening. This was her greatest opportunity yet to speak to voters—this time, a national audience. When the big evening arrived, Michelle was a bit nervous, but she was also confident. At this point, she knew every word of her speech by heart, having practiced it day after day.

In her speech, Michelle talked about her parents and the impact they had had on her life. Then she honored the 45th anniversary of Martin Luther King's famous "I Have a Dream" speech.

"I stand here today at the crosscurrents of that history," Michelle said, "knowing that my piece of the American dream is a blessing hard won by those who came before me. All of them driven by the same conviction that drove my dad to get up an hour early each day to painstakingly dress himself for work. The same conviction that drives the men and women I've met all across this country . . . I believe that each of us—no matter what our age or background or walk of life—each of us has something to contribute to the life of this nation. It's a belief Barack shares—a belief at the heart of his life's work."

Michelle went on to describe that "heart," a heart she knew so well. When she finished her speech, the convention crowd erupted in cheers, thousands of them waving signs that read, "Michelle." Seven-year-old Sasha and ten-year-old Malia came out on the stage, proudly hugging their mother. Behind Michelle and the girls, a screen appeared with Barack waving and smiling.

"Hey Daddy!" Sasha giggled into a microphone.

"Hey Sweetie!" Barack said back with a grin.

"Hello everyone!" Barack said to the cheering crowd. "How about Michelle Obama?"

The crowd roared its approval.

"Now you know why I asked her out so many times, even when she said no. You want a persistent president!"

During the three months that followed the Democratic National Convention, both Barack's and Michelle's popularity continued to build. The Republican nominee, John McCain, also tried using negative attacks, and once again that plan backfired. Eleven days before the presidential election, Michelle drew an enormous crowd in Akron, Ohio.

"We're just regular folks," she said of herself and Barack.

And in many ways they were. Michelle was the daughter of a blue-collar father and a stay-at-home mom. As the son of a struggling single mother, Barack had gone to live with his grandparents. Like so many Americans, these were two ordinary people who had worked hard, taken out loans to get through school, and barely managed at times to balance two careers while raising two children.

And yet Michelle also knew just how very extraordinary she and Barack were. What they were on the verge of achieving would be an outstanding chapter in American history: the first African American president and First Lady. But would Barack win? All the polls showed him leading John McCain, but nothing could be certain until the American people voted.

On election night, the Obamas and their daughters sat down to dinner at their home in Chicago. With them were Craig and his family and Marian Robinson. Marian asked her grandchildren about school and which teachers they liked best. The mood was low-key. Across the room, a television showed the returns coming in. It was looking more and more likely that Barack was going to win. Then the telephone rang, and Michelle walked over to answer it.

"Hello?" she said. She listened for a while, nodding. "Okay. Yes. Hold on one second."

Michelle put the phone down for a moment and looked across the room at her husband. Barack looked back, raising his eyebrows questioningly.

"Congratulations, Mr. President," she said with a wide smile.

Chapter 10

January 20, 2009, dawned cold and clear. Long before the sun streaked across the National Mall, the two-mile stretch of park that reaches from the Capitol to the Lincoln Memorial started to fill. By nine in the morning, more than a half million people had gathered. By eleven, some estimated the record-setting crowd to be close to two million people. It was a mass of humanity big enough to be seen from outer space. There had never been a larger crowd gathered at our nation's Capitol.

"Obama! Obama! Obama!"

The chant rolled like a wave from the steps of the Lincoln Memorial to the steps of the Capitol and then back again. With more than a million voices raised, some said that it felt like thunder shaking the very ground they stood upon.

"As far as you can see, everyone has the same expression," one reporter said. "It's more than celebration, more than gaiety. People are *happy*—so happy for this day."

As the noon hour grew closer, hundreds of thousands of American flags were held high. When it was time for Obama to take the presidential oath, Michelle, Malia, and Sasha stood beside him. Sasha was so small that she had to stand on top of a wooden box in order to see what was happening. A hush fell over the proud and excited crowd. In Michelle's hands was Abraham Lincoln's Bible, the Bible that Barack had personally chosen for the swearing-in oath. It was the first time the burgundy velvet Bible had been used since Lincoln himself had used it for his second inauguration in 1865. As Barack repeated the oath, Michelle smiled proudly at her husband. He had come so far so quickly. It was hard to believe that it had been not even twenty years since a young intern had walked into her office with a wide and honest smile. And now here stood that same man, the first African American president of the United States.

As the long day of parties, luncheons, and *ten* fancy balls came to an end, Michelle and Barack entered what would be their home for the next eight years—the White House. (Barack Obama would win a second term as president in 2012). Malia and Sasha had been asleep for hours in rooms that already contained all their belongings, clothes, and toys. Even the posters from their Chicago bedrooms hung on the walls. The White House staff had done their best to make Malia and Sasha feel at home.

Michelle quietly looked in on the girls. She worried about the changes suddenly taking place in their young lives, and she was determined to keep many of their day-to-day routines in place.

"The girls are going to do chores, so don't do everything," she had told the White House staff that afternoon. "They are making their beds and picking up their rooms on their own."

As the self-described "Mom-in-Chief," Michelle often pointed out that her most important job was raising her daughters to be well adjusted and thoughtful. She wanted their lives to be as normal as possible, though as Michelle toured their new home, she knew this would not always be easy. With a new home that contained a movie theater, game room, swimming pool, bowling alley, and 35 bedrooms, it was clear that Sasha and Malia's home life would be far from the norm. And outside of the home, millions of Americans were curious about the young Obama girls. Michelle and Barack quickly laid down strict rules to prevent the press from intruding into their girls' lives. They would decide when and where the girls could be photographed.

"Be seen, but not heard," was a rule the Obamas gave to Malia and Sasha early on. By this, they meant that the girls could smile and wave as much as they wanted at public functions, but that they should avoid speaking to the press. Michelle knew all too well how words, even innocent words from a child, could get twisted into rumors and lies.

And to help out, Marian Robinson finally moved out of the old apartment in Chicago and into the White House. This was the first time a grandparent had lived there. Known as "the First Grandma," she took the girls to school every morning and looked after them when Michelle had to be away. Malia and Sasha seemed to take all these changes in stride.

"They are more concerned about the dog we promised them than anything else right now," Michelle explained with a laugh.

Shortly after moving into the White House, Michelle and Barack kept their promise to their girls and got a fuzzy little puppy they named "Bo," after Barack Obama's initials.

Of course, besides being Mom-in-Chief, Michelle had another new and important job as First Lady of the United States. Nationwide, and even worldwide, people eagerly looked forward to seeing Michelle in this new role. Because of her beauty and style, Michelle was often compared to Jacqueline Kennedy, the glamorous wife of the 1960s president John F. Kennedy. Others thought that because of her law degree, intelligence, and devotion to young people, Michelle might be more like former First Lady Hillary Clinton. Still others compared Michelle to Eleanor Roosevelt who, as long ago as the 1930s, spoke out against poverty and racism. Eleanor also often told her husband, President Franklin D. Roosevelt, exactly what she thought about his decisions and what she thought he should do. Some Americans hoped Michelle would do this, but others complained that it would be a mistake.

"We don't need two presidents," one newspaper columnist insisted. "A First Lady should be a First Lady."

Michelle admired all of these past First Ladies, but she wasn't interested in being compared to any of them.

"It does me no good to spend my time as First Lady pretending to be something other than who I am," Michelle said in an interview. "I want us to talk honestly about the challenges we face. So that's what I bring that's unique from any other First Lady. I mean, I don't know any former First Ladies well enough to know how we compare—I can't make that comparison, but I know that this is who I am."

And from the very start, Michelle was indeed *herself*, a unique and hardworking First Lady who was passionate about the programs she created.

In 2010, Michelle gathered on the lawn behind the White House with a large group of children. Some of them giggled as she put a hula hoop around her waist and began spinning it.

"I can hula-hoop forever," Michelle shouted out to the kids.

The kids began counting how many times the First Lady spun the hula hoop. When Michelle got to nearly 150, she stopped and encouraged the children to try beating her number of spins. Suddenly, every child was moving, laughing, and spinning. This was all a part of a national program Michelle had named *Let's Move!* The point of the program was simple: Michelle wanted American children to get healthier through exercise and better diets.

"One in three American children are overweight or obese," Michelle pointed out. "So many children in this nation are facing health problems that are entirely preventable."

Michelle also commented that desserts and sweets were a rare treat in her home when she was growing up. Much of the food her own mother prepared was based on fresh fruits and vegetables.

"As a mother of two girls, I've often heard, 'I don't wanna eat it! It tastes bad!'" Michelle said. But Michelle insisted that there were all kinds of delicious and healthy ways to prepare vegetables. To prove her point, Michelle had the White House chefs prepare such snacks as zucchini quesadillas and spicy popcorn for the kids after they finished hula-hooping. All the vegetables for the snacks had come from a 1,100-square-foot garden that had been created on the South Lawn of the White House. There were even two big beehives for honey. With the help of two dozen fifth-graders, Michelle had planted corn, basil, zucchini, berries, spinach, and hot peppers, along with other fruits and vegetables. The "White House Garden" was only the second garden ever created by a First Lady. Michelle hoped that the garden might encourage American families to think about healthier eating as a way to slow down the obesity epidemic.

"And just because he's the leader of the free world does not excuse Barack from doing weeding in the garden," Michelle joked.

In addition to starting the *Let's Move!* program and the garden, Michelle often spoke out against the food industry. She argued against the ways that junk food and candy were advertised to children. She pointed out that the sugar content in much of the food that kids eat is far too high. And she worked to change what school cafeterias put on students' plates, including soft drinks, fried foods, and desserts. She encouraged schools—and families—to serve more juices, fruits and vegetables, and other healthy choices.

Naturally, there were those who complained about or made fun of the First Lady's efforts.

"Michelle Obama and her food police need to stay out of our lives and our kitchens," one writer complained.

"If my wife were First Lady," one Republican senator said, "she would let kids eat French fries again."

Conservative talk radio personality Rush Limbaugh called Michelle a "hypocrite" when she ate a dinner of ribs while on vacation. He then insulted her by saying that despite her talk about exercise and healthy food, she "does not project the image of women that you might see on the cover of the *Sports Illustrated* Swimsuit Issue."

And on a reality television show, Governor Sarah Palin was shown shopping for cookies. "This is in honor of Michelle Obama," she said with a smirk, "who said the other day that we should not have dessert!"

As always, Michelle ignored the haters and just kept on working. She was serious about her efforts, but she could also be lighthearted. On the *Ellen* show, Michelle outdid Ellen DeGeneres in a push-up challenge. Then on *The Tonight Show*, Michelle and host Jimmy Fallon competed in a fitness challenge that included dancing, tug-of-war, dodge ball, and a sack race. The First Lady won. Some people thought that it was undignified for the First Lady of the United States to be competing in a sack race or dancing on national television. Michelle didn't care.

"There's a method to my madness," she explained. "There's a reason why I've been out there jumping rope and hula-hooping and dancing to Beyoncé, whatever it takes. It's because I want kids to see that there are all kinds of ways to be active. And if I can do it, anybody can do it." In time, Michelle's hard work and positive attitude helped to bring about the passage of the Child Nutrition Bill. This bill helped ensure that the meals children received at school would be healthier. Michelle knew that better meals led to better concentration, brainpower, and success in school.

"Barack and I want our children—and all children in this nation—to know that the only limit to the height of your achievements is the reach of your dreams and your willingness to work hard for them," she had said in her speech at the Democratic National Convention. But she knew that many children's ability to work hard was damaged by poor nutrition and the health problems it caused. This is why she was so passionate about *Let's Move!*—and so successful.

In addition to helping children during Barack's first term as president, Michelle devoted herself to military veterans and their families. She and the vice president's wife, Jill Biden, named this program *Joining Forces*. Both Michelle and Jill were concerned about the families of those serving in the military. Too often, they realized, Americans didn't know how difficult life could be for the loved ones of soldiers serving overseas.

Michelle discovered that many spouses lived in fear of getting news that their husband or wife had been killed.

"A good day is when a military chaplain doesn't knock on my door," one woman told Michelle.

This was an eye-opener. The more Michelle and Jill talked to the spouses and loved ones of soldiers, the more they realized how much many families suffered. Because families had to move around to different military locations, spouses often made less money at jobs, had fewer friends, and lacked a strong support network. No one had ever paid much attention to this problem, but Michelle did.

"When our troops serve, their families are serving too," Michelle said. "It's time to do our part. It's not enough just to feel grateful. It's time for each of us to act."

Michelle Obama's genuine concern for American people made her popularity soar during Barack's first term. Sometimes Barack joked that his wife was far more popular than he was. For Michelle, her new job as First Lady was exciting—mostly because it gave her an opportunity to make a difference, to help people. This had been her dream since she had been a ten-year-old kid talking to Craig about kids at school who were being bullied, making poor grades, or not getting enough to eat. Sometimes the problems of others had kept her awake. Now she could do something about them.

"Wow, what an opportunity," Michelle said on the *Larry King Live* television show. "What a privilege it is to have the opportunity to speak to people's hearts, to be a part of moving this country in a different direction."

In part, that "different direction" would mean, Michelle hoped, a more welcoming and inclusive country. Perhaps now, with the first African American president, our country could begin to come together more fully. If we could talk about racism and deal with it in an open and honest way, Michelle often noted, perhaps we could begin to move past it. Finally.

Many Americans were hopeful. Yet there were people who, as Michelle rose ever higher, were determined to bring her down. And some would stoop to astounding lows in their attempts to do it.

Chapter 11

*I*n Virginia, a well-known school board member sent out an email to coworkers and friends. The email included a picture of shirtless African women dancing with members of their tribe. It was the kind of picture one might see in a travel magazine.

"This is Michelle Obama's high-school reunion," he wrote below the picture.

At a rodeo in California, an announcer joked that a prominent senator's wife was offered $250,000 to pose in *Playboy*. Then he went on to say that the best Michelle could get was a $50 offer from *National Geographic*.

When a gorilla escaped from a South Carolina zoo, a former Republican elections official went on Facebook and posted, "I'm sure it's just one of Michelle's ancestors—probably harmless."

On the Internet, where any coward could post something anonymously, the insults were constant.

Michelle's ugly like that chimp from Planet of the Apes.

She shouldn't be wearing sleeveless dresses! Show some respect!

Michelle Obama needs to learn her place and stop being so uppity.

Much of this hate and cruelty was based in either racism or sexism. Sadly, there were plenty of people who were upset and angry at Michelle simply because of her skin color or because she was a woman. In the past, there had always been criticisms of First Ladies, but no president's wife had ever had to endure such vicious insults. Michelle would not give the haters the satisfaction of letting them know that their words stung. She held her head high and moved forward.

"One of the lessons that I grew up with was to always stay true to yourself and never let what somebody else says distract you from your goals," Michelle told a magazine interviewer. "And so when I hear about negative or false attacks, I really don't invest any energy in them, because I know who I am."

Michelle often considered how far America had come. It was a very different place from the country that had legally allowed her great-great grandfather to be enslaved. In only a handful of generations, African Americans had gone from bondage to freedom to equal rights. And now Americans had even elected an African American president for two terms. So much had changed, but there was still so much to do. Michelle believed that Americans were often reluctant to face racism head-on and *really* talk about it, because that was hard. It was uncomfortable. Some Americans preferred to believe that racism no longer existed simply because laws had changed. But Michelle knew that no law could change the hearts and minds of those who still thought it was okay to discriminate. She felt that Americans still had a lot of work to do when it came to racism, and she wasn't afraid to say so.

"This stuff is deep, and we haven't touched it as a nation," Michelle said in an MSNBC interview. "We don't deal with pain that has been caused by racism and division. And then we're surprised when it rears its head among whites and blacks. We haven't dealt with it, and it's hurting all of us. We can't afford to have generations of children of any race believing they can't be exactly who they think they should be."

Some people accused Michelle of creating more tension. They claimed that *she* was racist for saying that we still had race issues in our country. There were those who claimed that the United States had not really had problems between blacks and whites until the Obamas entered the White House. Michelle knew how untrue that was. As always, she placed her hope for real change in the young people of our nation. Michelle was a much in-demand speaker for both high-school and college graduations, and she often spoke to the young graduates about their duty to challenge racism.

"As you go forth, when you encounter folks

who still hold the old prejudices because they've only been around folks like themselves; when you meet folks who think they know all the answers because they've never heard any other viewpoints, it's up to *you* to help them see things differently," she said in a 2014 speech to high-school graduates in Topeka, Kansas.

This concern for and faith in young people inspired two of Michelle's programs during Barack's second term. Growing up, Michelle had often known kids on the South Side of Chicago who, unlike her, never even considered going to college. Their families were often too poor to afford college. And many of these young people never dared dream that they might pursue higher education. Some thought they didn't "belong" in college or that they weren't good enough. This mindset of defeat of so many young people from low-income families upset Michelle sometimes to the point of tears. It seemed so unfair.

In response, Michelle started a new program called *Reach Higher*, which encouraged high-school graduates to do just that—to reach for higher education at either a community college or a four-year college. In 1990, the United States had ranked first in the world for college graduates aged 25–34. In 2014, that ranking had dropped to 12th place. As more families struggled to make ends meet and college became more expensive, many young people simply gave up. Michelle was determined to turn that around. She and Barack set a challenge and a goal for the young people of America: ranking first in the world again by 2020.

"Make a plan to advance yourselves," she told a crowd of high-school students at an inner-city school. "Study for college assessment tests. Ask for help, not just once, but again and again."

Michelle looked out at the sea of young and often discouraged faces. Some of the kids looked skeptical.

"Do you hear what I'm telling you?" she said in a louder and more urgent voice. "I'm giving you some insights that a lot of rich kids all over the country already know, and I want you to know it too, because you have got to go and get your education. You have *got* to! If anyone is telling you that you're not college material—*anyone*—prove them wrong."

Then, near the end of her time as First Lady, Michelle became concerned about a worldwide problem with education. Far too many girls in poorer countries were receiving no education at all. In some countries, men did not think women needed an education. In other places, schools did not exist or were too far away, making it dangerous for a young girl to walk to school. And sometimes girls were forced to marry at a young age, making education impossible.

Michelle thought these practices were wrong. She knew that education would make the lives of women and their families better. In time, it could even transform entire countries. For too long, poor countries had remained in a cycle of poverty due to a lack of education for many of their citizens. Michelle was determined to help bring about change.

"I see myself in these girls, I see my daughters in these girls, and I simply cannot walk away from them," Michelle said in 2015.

In the summer of 2016, what could be considered the most unusual race for the presidency in the history of the United States was taking place. The Republicans had nominated billionaire businessman and reality television star Donald Trump. Trump had never held office and had no political experience. On the other side, the Democrats had nominated former First Lady, New York senator, and Secretary of State Hillary Clinton. She was the first woman to ever be nominated by a major party for president. The two candidates could not have been less alike.

Many Americans believed that Trump would not even stand a chance in the primary race. In debates, he was often rude, calling his opponents names and making personal attacks on them. At his rallies, he made insulting comments about Latinos, Muslims, and even a disabled reporter from the *New York Times*. In the past, he had referred to women as "fat pigs," "dogs," and "slobs," and had often judged women based solely on their looks. He had illegally blocked black people from living in buildings he owned. And in what many Americans considered the ultimate example of racism, Trump had long insisted that Barack Obama, the first black president, should not be president at all. Trump falsely claimed that Obama had not been born in America. Even after Obama proved that he had been born in Hawaii, Trump continued to claim that Obama's birth certificate was fake.

And yet, Trump struck a chord with many Americans. Some felt that it was time to shake up "politics as usual." Some admired an outspoken businessman who, in their opinion, was speaking his mind; he wasn't just another politician reading from a script.

"He says it like it is," one Trump supporter explained. "He's not always worried about being politically correct."

Trump's slogan was "Make America Great Again." In many towns in rural parts of America, things were far from great. Some people in these depressed towns thought politicians in Washington were to blame. They felt that the federal government had ignored them for years. Trump promised these people that he'd be different, that he would make their small towns great again. Many of these people longed for anyone in power to be on their side. They believed Trump's promises.

To the surprise of many, though not to his fans, Donald Trump won the Republican primary by a landslide. Now the race for the presidency was between Hillary Clinton and Trump.

As the campaign wore on, Democrats (and even many Republicans) became increasingly alarmed by Trump's words and actions. He encouraged violence against protestors at his rallies. He insulted the parents of a fallen soldier because they were Muslim. He suggested that women who had abortions should be punished. And Trump's choice for his vice president was a man who was fierce in his fight against gay rights and same-sex marriage. He vowed to build a wall to keep Mexican immigrants out of the U.S.

"How low can Trump go?" one magazine article asked, pointing out that never before had a presidential candidate been such a bully.

Michelle Obama had wondered the same thing. As a mother, Michelle had always taught her daughters to be kind and thoughtful. Under no circumstances should they ever bully and insult others who were different. She worried about the kind of message Donald Trump was sending to young people. In addition, Michelle did not agree with many of Trump's ideas. Walls to keep people out and banning people from the U.S. based on their religious beliefs did not seem in keeping with American ideals.

So when asked if she would speak at the 2016

Democratic National Convention, Michelle did not hesitate to say yes.

Michelle spoke about her daughters that evening at the convention. She talked about how she and Barack had worried about their little girls when they had first moved into the White House nearly eight years earlier.

"I realized that our time at the White House would form the foundation for who they would become, and how well we managed this experience could truly make or break them. That is what Barack and I think about every day as we try to guide and protect our girls through the challenges of this unusual life in the spotlight—how we urge them to ignore those who question their father's citizenship or faith. How we insist that the hateful language they hear from public figures on TV does not represent the true spirit of this country. How we explain that when someone is cruel, or acts like a bully, you don't stoop to their level. No, our motto is, *when they go low, we go high*."

With her typical style, intensity, and humor, Michelle managed to give one of the most compelling and convincing speeches of the entire convention. Without ever even saying Trump's name, she made vividly clear the differences between her values and his. And she assured the crowd and the millions of Americans watching that these were Hillary Clinton's values, too. Although the primary race between Barack and Hillary in

2008 had been rocky at times, Michelle had always admired Clinton.

"I think the world of Hillary Clinton," Michelle had told a newspaper reporter. "She is one of the most successful and powerful and groundbreaking women on this planet."

In the months leading up to the election, Michelle Obama would become one of Clinton's most valuable supporters. Her upbeat speeches in support of Clinton drew thousands of voters. As always, Michelle focused on the positives of Clinton rather than the negatives of Trump. But then, on October 7, just a month before the election, something happened that changed Michelle's typically positive campaign speech. A 2005 recording of Donald Trump bragging about sexually assaulting women was released. In the recording, Trump claimed that because he is famous, he "can do anything" to women.

Millions of Americans were stunned and sickened—including Michelle Obama.

"I have to tell you that I can't stop thinking about this," Michelle said to a crowd in New Hampshire, her voice shaking with anger. "It has shaken me to my core in a way that I couldn't have predicted."

She pointed out that it was beyond unbelievable that a candidate for President of the United States had made these comments.

"This is not something we can ignore,"

Michelle continued. "It is cruel. It is frightening. And the truth is, it hurts. . . . This is not normal. This is disgraceful. It is intolerable. And it doesn't matter what party you belong to. . . . No woman deserves to be treated this way. None of us deserve this kind of abuse."

Michelle told the crowd that a Trump victory would send out a message to children "that bigotry and bullying are perfectly acceptable in the leader of the country."

Michelle had devoted her eight years as First Lady to making the lives of young people better. Now she feared that the messages Trump sent out and many of the plans he claimed he would carry out as president would hurt the lives of these same young people. In the final weeks leading up to the election, Michelle worked harder than ever to help Hillary Clinton get elected. Many Americans assumed that after Trump's comments, Clinton would win fairly easily.

But they were wrong. On November 8, Donald Trump pulled off what many consider the greatest presidential election upset in American history.

Michelle looked out at a roomful of young people a week after the election.

"Don't ever lose hope," she said quietly with a smile. "Don't ever feel fear. You belong here—you got that? Keep working hard, because it is going to be so important now to be educated and focused."

In the back of the room, a student called out, "Will you run for president in 2020, please?"

Michelle just laughed and joked, "Be quiet back there."

Since the moment Trump had been elected, social media had exploded with talk of Michelle being a future candidate under the hashtag #Michelle2020. But Michelle had long said that she wasn't interested in running for any political office.

"No, no, and nope. Not going to do it," Michelle had responded in early 2016 when asked if she'd ever run for president. Her plans, she said, were to continue serving the American people: Democrats, Republicans, everyone.

After the election, more than ever before, Michelle stressed that we are *one* country. In spite of our sometimes very strong differences, we are all Americans—and there is still so very much work to do.

"The world as it is just won't do," Michelle had once stated. "We have an obligation to fight for the world as it should be. That is the thread that connects our hearts."

In the spirit of her great-grandfather who, against all odds, taught himself to read, and in the spirit of her own father who, despite pain and illness, kept an optimistic outlook, Michelle has chosen to keep moving forward. She has chosen to believe that the best is yet to come.